RURAL KENT

Maidstone, fifteenth-century tithe barn

RURAL KENT

by *JOHN BOYLE*
with drawings by JOHN L. BERBIERS

ROBERT HALE & COMPANY   *LONDON*

ISBN 0 7091 5370 8

Robert Hale & Company
Clerkenwell House
Clerkenwell Green
London, EC1

*Filmset by Specialised Offset Services Ltd., Liverpool
and printed and bound in Great Britain by
Redwood Burn Limited, Trowbridge & Esher*

Contents

Illustrations

Acknowledgements

Acknowledgements by authors seem to be of various patterns, some formal, some chatty, and some merely perfunctory. These are intended to be, if only for a change, candid.

When researching for a book, one is bound to be something of a nuisance to various people, and there will occasionally be those (I think I had dealings with three) who will not hesitate to let one know this. All the deeper, therefore, is my gratitude to the vast majority who have shown that kindness and interest which have made my forays into the Kent countryside such a pleasure, nay, a delight.

To all these good people, and to those who have assisted in other ways, I express my sincere thanks. It would be invidious to give a list of names, because someone would almost certainly be left out. I must, however, mention the help of the Rev. Canon S. Graham Brade-Birks, D.Sc., F.S.A., Vicar of Godmersham with Crundale. He read through the typescript, and by his suggestions saved me from perpetrating a number of serious heresies, not, I hasten to say, in matters of religious faith, but about the geology and social history of the Weald. He also disentangled for me some very complicated knots in the story of Jane Austen's family connections with Godmersham. Lastly, he offered some caustic comments on *my* caustic comments – I only wish I were allowed to print some of them.

I gratefully acknowledge Dr Brade-Birks's help and encouragement.

Hollingbourne village

Introduction

No one who writes about rural Kent (which is my brief) can ignore the mystique with which the county is invested. It has a voluminous folklore; moreover a preconceived image, often highly coloured, will I suspect exist in the minds of many readers.

The folklore varies from harmless exaggeration (The Garden of England) to downright falsehood (Canterbury's Westgate saved by the casting vote of the mayor); from the nocturnal goings-on of Father Time in the churchyard at Cranbrook, which are a mere joke, to the county motto – *Invicta* (Unconquered) – which not a few inhabitants think is the name of their White Horse, but which *we*, presumably, are meant to take seriously.

Many people have a highly idealistic conception of Kent. It is also a county much written about and eulogized, much drawn, painted and photographed, usually under the most favourable conditions. Take Aylesford as an example. You have probably seen the conventional glossy, brightly coloured photograph showing the medieval bridge and the gabled roofs, with the church brooding over them, and the whole reflected in the smooth waters of the River Medway: but when you visit Aylesford you may well find that it is neither brightly coloured nor glossy; that the tide is out, and instead of a stretch of water reflecting the bridge and village you have banks of grey, slimy mud; that the point from which the photograph was taken is a miry park full of motor lorries on a stretch of the river bank between the nice photogenic stone bridge and a very nasty steel-girdered counterpart; and that, anyhow, this oasis of charm is girded around within half a mile by huge factories and warehouses. For the guidebook photographer the sun always shines, and summer is perpetual, but reality is more changeable. There are many months when, instead of blossom and wild flowers, the earth bears the chevron imprint of the farmer's tractor in the mud; when the unpruned fruit trees with only an occasional shrivelled leaf to jig madly in the cruel wind resemble not the demure bridesmaids of the poet's fancy, but rather endless rows of Shock-Headed Peters.

But the real Kent is much more interesting than the ideal one. At Aylesford, for instance, when you have recovered from the shock, and perhaps blamed the camera – for not exactly lying, but not telling the whole truth either – you can wander round the narrow streets, go into the church, and visit the Friars, and find all sorts of things there that do not appear on the photograph but are really ten times more interesting than you ever hoped.

And in the winter countryside the new-turned furrow and the sprouting winter wheat relieve the monotony of woods black except for the evergreen holly and ivy and fir-tree; once you have got a taste for it this landscape has a quiet and subdued beauty which makes the rioting colours of spring and summer seem gaudy by contrast.

Enjoying a real Kent, and not an imaginary one, has some practical bonuses, too: the pub where the beer is specially good, or where they serve real cream with the lunchtime cherry tart; the village shop well stocked with goods the town is short of, or displaying perhaps some domestic item one has been looking for in vain for months; even the convent where the kindly nuns sell, as a side-line, and ridiculously cheap, religious gewgaws that make splendid little presents for children. And the woods and hedgerows produce in spring the tiny wild flowers whose sweetness no camera can capture or words describe; in autumn the earthier delights of blackberries and cobnuts.

Most important of all, for every folktale that a writer may be compelled to question there are a score of much more surprising but true stories worth recalling; and for every Kentish scene that is well known to the point of becoming hackneyed there are a hundred that deserve more attention than they now receive.

Having thus perhaps cleared the ground, where and how does one begin to build? Fortunately, Kent has not only folklore and preconceptions; it has also salutary precedents, better probably than those of any other county. The two great stalwarts William Lambarde in the sixteenth century and Edward Hasted at the end of the eighteenth prefaced their explorations of Kent with some general remarks on the county as a whole. Lambarde described his investigations as a 'perambulation', and The Perambulator he has remained ever since. His book, written in the reign of Queen Elizabeth I, was the first county history ever. Two centuries later, Edward Hasted devoted the greater part of his life and fortune to producing a work filling (second edition) twelve volumes, and entitled a *History and Topographical Survey of the County of Kent*. It is still popular and indispensible. His name should be, but rarely is, pronounced Hay-sted. What was good enough for Lambarde and Hasted is certainly good enough for me, and I follow, with fitting humility, in their footsteps;

Teston bridge

so my first two chapters are a general introduction to the county.

When they came down to detail, my two distinguished exemplars had rather different ideas. A zealous, if not over-zealous, partisan of the Reformation, the Elizabethan Lambarde nevertheless based his perambulation on the ecclesiastical set-up which had survived that cataclysm, taking first the diocese of Canterbury, roughly East Kent, and then that of Rochester, the western part, going round the edge of each in a clockwise direction and ending with a description of what was left in the middle. Hasted, in the late eighteenth century, founding his order on administrative divisions, lathes and hundreds, worked across from west to east, from Deptford to the Isle of Thanet; only at the strictly local level did he proceed on a church-ordained path as he moved, within the hundred, from parish to parish.

I intend to rely, with a certain amount of give and take, on natural and geographical divisions. Most of the county can quite easily be thus divided as follows:

The north coast
The south-east coast
Romney Marsh
The North Downs
Darent and Medway valleys
Stour valley
The Quarry Hills
The Weald
The Surrey border
The new Canterbury

13

I now come to the most delicate part of this Introduction. There lurks in every true Kentish heart the suspicion that to write properly, or even properly write about the county one should be Kent born and bred; this sentiment is unconsciously displayed by the composers of dust-jacket blurbs and in criticisms of books about the county: "Mr X has the advantage of having been brought up in Kent ..." "Mr Z, unlike the earlier writer on this subject, Mr Y, is not a native of the county, and therefore some allowance must be made ..."

Neither John Berbiers nor I come from Kent, but we shall not behave as the Scotchman James Boswell did at his first meeting with Dr Johnson and cringingly complain that "we cannot help it"; on the other hand we shall try to avoid gross errors such as those made by a much-favoured Kentish writer when he placed Boughton Aluph in the Weald, referred to a mythical Boughton Winchelsea, and placed them, and Boughton Malherbe, "roughly half-way between the North and South Downs"!

I recall that some years ago, at a function in the University at Canterbury, I was dilating upon the city's problems to a receptive listener when unexpectedly, one of the highest dignitaries of the county bore down upon us and spoke a few words in my companion's ear.

"I know this man," said his lordship; "don't you believe a word he says!"

This was his kindly way of admitting that, although a Yorkshireman by birth, I could now be considered practically a member of the Kent family. As the message that I am trying to get across, especially to Kent readers, I cannot improve on his sentiment. Do not believe a word I say, but go out and test it on the spot, in the countryside of Kent. It should take you quite a long time, but you will enjoy every minute of it.

For those who live far from Kent, I can only say that they will have to take my word for what is said in this book, and *all* readers can be comforted by the thought that the pictures at least are 'true likenesses'.

Brenchley village

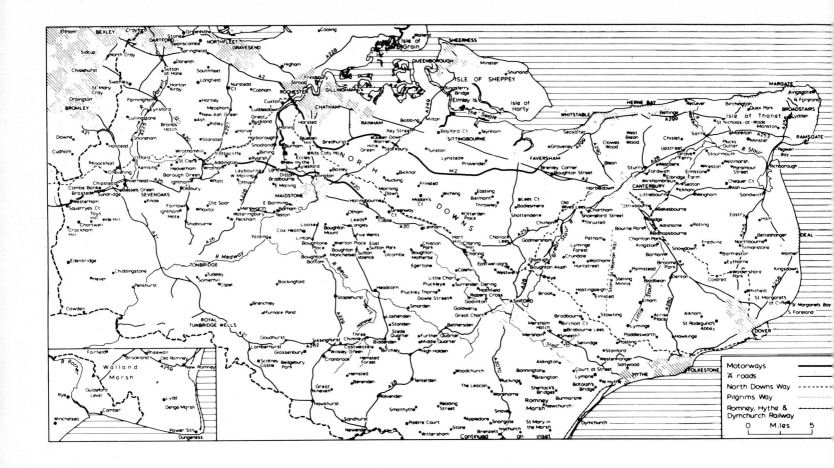

Motorways
'A' roads
North Downs Way
Pilgrims Way
Romney, Hythe &
Dymchurch Railway

0   Miles   5

CHAPTER ONE

White Horse In – Or Out

A civil servant once told me that in his department Kent was divided into three parts – Metropolitan Kent, Estuarial Kent and Feudal Kent. I don't suppose that this classification was used in official letters and circulars; nor can I safely adopt it for present purposes. The word 'feudal', while it would probably make the preservationists purr, would ruffle the feelings of those Kent patriots who see the county as the torch-bearer of Progress; and I can quite see that modish places like Folkestone, Tunbridge Wells, and even New Ash Green would not like it either.

I imagine that all of the civil servants' 'feudal' Kent is included in my brief, while their 'metropolitan' Kent is not; it has been taken into Greater London now, and very little of it is rural, anyhow – a small area round Downe and Cudham, and a short run of 'metropolitan green belt'. Of the third category, 'estuarial' Kent, very little is rural: Dartford and Gravesend, Gillingham, Chatham and Strood have all become almost wholly industrial, and not very suitable for pictorial description, although Hasted was impressed with the chalk working along the Thames, and with the far-flung trade in it, even to Holland and Flanders; and later writers have added a touch of Dante's *Inferno* to their accounts of Northfleet, Stone, Greenhithe and Swanscombe. Rochester and Maidstone are industrial too, but we shall have something to say about them, no doubt.

The last hundred years or so of the county's history is that of one long rearguard action against the encroachment of London. To understand why this has been so, one has only to compare the state of the parishes of the old Kent that bordered on London with that of the same places today. The Kent of Hasted began at Deptford, the deep ford over the River Ravensbourne, and Kent House near Beckenham was the first house in Kent to be seen by the traveller coming from 'Surry'. Deptford was four miles from London, and Lewisham "a most agreeable and convenient recess for opulent merchants".

Greenwich was reckoned "one of the genteelest and pleasantest towns in England; many of its inhabitants being persons of rank and fortune ... The dryness and salubrity of the soil and air, the conveniency of the park,

Eltham Palace, roof

built village". Eltham's nearness to the metropolis "and the healthiness and pleasantness of its situation" made it "much resorted to by merchants and people of fortune, for their summer residence, either in their houses or in handsome lodgings". Its palace was a sad loss to Kent — kings had held their court there and parliaments had deliberated.

By 1888, however, all these places had become just like the rest of London, both geographically and in the chaos and inadequacy of the administration; so Parliament stepped in and created the London County Council, in which they were at once included. Whether Kent made a fight of it I don't know; it was a little before my time. But this, unfortunately, was not the end; suburbia continued to sprawl over Beckenham, Bromley and Bexley, Chislehurst and Orpington, the Crays and Sidcup, and over Erith and Crayford, with the result that in 1963 there was another surgical operation: Greater London was invented and Kent contributed about a third of its own population and rateable value to the new Frankenstein's monster.

This time there was a great row. Opponents said that the changes were a political move by the Tory Government to wrest London out of the grip of the Labour party by bringing the suburban legions to the rescue. Another cynical suggestion was that it was a

the general pleasantness of the adjoining country, and its near neighbourhood to the metropolis, contribute to make it a most desirable residence for people of fashion and fortune."

Blackheath was "a beautiful plain lying on the south side of Greenwich park" and Charlton "a pleasant well-

18

public relations exercise to make London sound bigger in its competition with foreign cities like New York and Tokyo. Be that as it may, the people who lived in Bromley and the other places, or most of them, seemed, to the distress of the Kent County Council, to regard the idea of the loss of their status as Kentish men and Fair Maids almost with indifference. This was what knocked the stuffing out of the opposition; the rest of the county had no stomach for a grandstand fight to the finish to rescue people who did not particularly want to be saved.

Suburban though they may be, if these places had stayed Kentish I should have had to make more than a passing reference to some of their architectural treasures. As it is I can only bid a sorrowful farewell to Bexley's thirteenth-century church and its Elizabethan house, altered in Stuart times, Hall Place; Bexleyheath's Danson Park and its two Victorian masterpieces, the Red House and Christ Church; Bromley's Sundridge Park and Holwood; Keston's archaeological sites. And to Downe, and Cudham which are rural still; only the invisible line drawn by the politician excludes them from our subject-matter – rural Kent. But the faithful Post Office, whether from heroic obstinacy or from sheer inertia, we know not, still regards all the places torn away in 1965 as part of Kent.

Within less than ten years there came another

Sundridge Park, Bromley

convulsion, the attempt to 'reorganize' local government. I might be accused of having an axe to grind if I gave my candid opinion about this exercise, but I can at least say that there are those – and, as the inflated rate demands come in, they seem to be growing in number – who consider the result disastrous, costing, at a time of financial danger, untold millions to achieve nil,

Red House, Bexleyheath

or more probably minus, results. This reform played havoc with the local authorities within Kent, but the county itself did better than most. When in some parts of the country great and famous shires were being hacked out of recognition in the name of local government reorganization, Kent kept its name and preserved its boundaries and, in fact, without asking or even desiring such a result, had the ancient City, County of a City and County Borough of Canterbury added to it. As long ago as 1461 Edward IV had promised Canterbury that it would remain separate and distinct from the county of Kent "for ever", and for half a millennium kings and queens, good and bad, of every dynasty, and governments of every political hue, had respected Edward's promise. How ironical that it should be a 'Conservative' government, led by a Kentish politician, that should contemptuously dishonour King Edward's scrap of parchment.

Under the new set-up, which includes such strange counties as Greater Manchester, the West Midlands, and Humberside, Kent was left, with Hampshire, as one of the two leading counties of the old style – shires if you like. Now, two or three 'metropolitan' counties are more populous and wealthy, and in sheer area Kent is now left well behind by many of the composite creations such as Cumbria and unpronounceable places in Wales.

Not satisfied with swallowing large chunks of Kent, London continues to make its presence felt over what remains. Patches of commuter country are found all the way to the limits of the county, eastward to the Thanet towns and southwards to Tunbridge Wells. The inner ring includes Dartford, Swanley, Otford and Kemsing, with Sevenoaks, almost suburban but manfully striving to keep its ancient personality, just a little further out. The Darent valley, to the south 'of Dartford, lives precariously; apart from Otford and Kemsing, major development has leapfrogged over it to Longfield and Meopham. Wherever in Kent there is a good train service to town, there will the commuters be gathered together. Southern Electric (as it used to be called) has carried the commuters all over the county; even in the heart of the Weald they have their little colonies, a Weald once almost uninhabited. And Kent is blocked off from the Midlands and north and east England by the sprawling mass of the capital, with no satisfactory way round, and the various roads through a lengthy and tedious mental torture.

Physically, someone once described the county as being like a fist sticking out towards the Continent. The outline of Kent is not really at all like a fist, and its role in history and before that in prehistory has been that of receiving rather than handing out the blows of invasion.

21

The coastline of Kent can best be described as being, like the taste of salt, *characteristic*. The terrain of the county is so varied that we can without effort divide it up geographically if we wish to do so. Of the northern estuarial tract we have already heard. Another low-lying section is Romney Marsh at the southern end. Our historians wax gloomily eloquent about the agues, fevers and noxious vapours of these ill-favoured regions, which the Perambulator Lambarde considered to offer wealth without health:

> And therefore very reasonable is their conceite [said Lambarde] which doe imagine that Kent hath three steps, or degrees, of which the first (they say) offereth Wealth without health: the second, giveth both Wealth and health: and the thirde affoordeth Health onely, and little or no Wealth. For, if a man, minding to passe through Kent toward London, should arrive and make his first step on land in Rumney Marshe, he shall rather finde good grasse under foote, than wholesome Aire above the head: againe, if he step over the Hilles and come into the Weald, he shall have at once the commodities both of the Aire, and of the Earth: But if he passe that, and climbe the next step of hilles that are betweene him and London, he shall have wood, conies, and corn, for his wealth, and (toward the increase of his health) if he seeke, he shall finde a good stomacke in the stonie field.

Romney Marsh, and the lands bordering the Thames estuary, were in fact afflicted with endemic malaria.

Today they are no doubt just as healthy as other parts of Kent.

Lambarde's "hilles that are between him and London" are the North Downs, very aptly called the backbone of Kent. To explain the creation of the Downs, and the Weald which Lambarde mentions as his "second degree", we have to go back millions of years to the time when Kent, and nearby Sussex, like most of what is now England, were at the bottom of a great sea and, as most people have read, the shells and bones of marine life gradually built up layers of chalk that are such an important feature of the geology of these counties. As the waters receded, the chalk, and the underlying layers of clay, gault, flints, greensand, and sedimentary rock (a good 5,000 feet thickness of miscellaneous geology), were pushed up in the form of a dome, which according to one account went on swelling until, with a mighty crack, it split down the middle; or according to another, did not exactly split, but, due to the Kent (and Sussex) weather, or more probably the wave action of the retreating ocean, gradually wore away. Whatever the cause, the effect was the same: at first a mighty chasm was created with steep sides of chalk; as the erosion went on, these sides insensibly — we are speaking in terms of millions of years — got further and further away from each other until the chasm became a broad vale, growing

Goudhurst High Street

ever broader until its sides were far distant, as distant, in fact, as Dover is from Eastbourne. These two sundered masses of soft white rock finally consolidated as the North and South Downs, and the floor of the valley between them became the Weald. The effect was similar to that of slicing the side off a hard-boiled egg after the shell has been removed: you will have white round the sides corresponding to the North and South Downs, with the yellow yolk in the middle which is the Weald with its clay. The South Downs come no further than Beachy Head in Sussex where they are cut off by the waters of the Channel, but the North Downs continue right through Kent from the Greater London border at Halstead to the South Foreland, before the sea terminates them. Because of these happenings of millions of years ago the North Downs, a tilted slab, rise gently from the level of the Thames and its estuary to a height of some six to eight hundred feet at the escarpment, which overlooks the Weald stretching away to the south.

I hope I am not getting too technical, because there is now a slight complication to explain, that of the quarry or stone hills. You see, there are the other strata to be considered, the layer called by the geologists the greensand, which is wedged between the clay and the chalk; and the impressively-named Hastings beds, a sort of sandstone, so that when the great split occurred there

was, if we go back to the example of the egg, a line – a green line if you like – between the white and the yolk; perhaps we should have made it a duck egg. This is the reason why, between the deep escarpment of the Downs and the beginning of the Weald proper, there lies the greensand ridge, nothing like as high as the Downs but producing the well-known building stone called Kentish rag. The ridge has no name on the map, but our old friend Hasted called it "the sand, or quarry hills", while the moderns refer to it also as the 'stone hills'.

But what of the Hastings beds? Well, unfortunately, this is where the simile of the sliced egg breaks down – unless you imagine that the hen had swallowed a stone which found its way into the middle of the egg. These beds in fact lay below the Wealden clay, and where the height of the geological dome was, halfway between the North and South Downs, they resisted the erosion better, and were left to form a ridge, coming to its height around Crowborough in Sussex, and running through into Kent to create the varied scenery of the High Weald round Goudhurst and Brenchley.

Well-known places on the quarry hills are Sevenoaks and Chartwell, while local people tend to think first of Boughton Monchelsea, near Maidstone, where some of the principal quarries for the Kentish rag are, or were, found. Southward from the quarry hills the Weald of

Kent stretches away to the Sussex border.

The word 'Weald' means 'a wooded place' – compare the German *Wald*. Right into historical times it was sparsely inhabited, except by hogs which came or were brought by their owners to eat the acorns and beechmast. In Kent it begins at the summit of the quarry hills, or in some places at the foot of their southern slopes. Sussex by contrast seems to include everything north of the *South Downs* as part of the Weald of Sussex.

Kent is a happy hunting ground for the archaeologist. Before about 6000 BC Britain was joined to the Continent, and tribes from either could wander to and fro at will. When the sea broke through and formed the Channel it seems that the travellers could not shake off their old ways and, taking to boats, continued to make their visits. As our national character began to develop, and the people cut off in Britain became more and more distrustful of foreigners, these incursions took on the aspect of hostile invasions, and it was Kent, or Cantium as the Romans called it, that usually bore the first shock of the successive human waves that flooded over Britain. The present county is, in consequence, littered with the flotsam and jetsam of past and gone civilizations – palaeolithic tools in the gravels of the Thames, Stour and Medway; remains of Neolithic and Bronze Age barrows scattered far inland and megalithic remains like Kit's

Reculver

Coty House, around the Medway valley; Celtic hillforts such as Oldbury near Ightham; and earthworks of the invading Belgae like Bigberry (or Bigbury) near Canterbury. The Romans built forts at Reculver and Richborough, both still there to see. The remains of the one at Dover are not visible but the pharos or lighthouse, perhaps the most interesting Roman structure in Britain,

25

still stands on the cliffs within the walls of the Norman castle.

No county has a richer heritage of ancient churches, and there are fragmentary remains of seventh-century date in at least ten of them, and bits and pieces of Saxon work built into the later walls of a score of others. The entries in Domesday Book suggest that many more Kent villages had churches in Saxon times but your Saxon was, as it has been put, a carpenter rather than a mason, and his buildings were usually wooden. It was left to the Normans to cover the county with stone-built village churches. So many of these date from the twelfth and thirteenth centuries that for a parish to have a church seven or eight hundred years old is nothing remarkable at all.

However unwelcome their over-efficient presence may have been, the Normans certainly gave England a new architectural deal. They also gave Kent its two cathedrals, sweeping away whatever was there before, and began the series of castles and fortified houses that continued up to Tudor times.

A couple of hundred years ago social conditions in Kent were startlingly different from those of today. An example can be found in the carefully elaborated distinctions which separated the small minority of gentlemen from the rest of the population, and the subtle

rules which determined the quantity of wealth and the length of the probationary period which would enable a farming family to develop in course of time into gentry; and the requisite scale of transaction which would promote a person from the mean and degrading condition of a tradesman to the genteel status of a merchant adventurer. But the very existence of these rules was regarded as a concession to modernity; under the feudal system it was an actionable wrong for a knightly guardian to allow his ward to marry anybody who had the degradation of even living in a borough.

Yet this same Kent could produce from periods even earlier, startling parallels with things of today. Nothing seems further removed from the smiling countryside of Kent than the horrors of a concentration camp, yet the pleasant village of Bockingfold some hundreds of years ago went under its original name Buckenwald. This came to light when King Edward I got wind of the fact that the local inhabitants were making free of his game preserves and came down to Buckenwald to read the medieval equivalent of the Riot Act.

Again, eighteenth-century writers carefully listed the plants that grew in the hedgerows of the county and it is surprising to read amongst them of cannabis in Southfleet and spearmint at Maidstone.

The problem of squatters was not unknown, and the

methods then adopted could perhaps with advantage be copied by presentday sufferers. The premises were the unfinished mansion of the Cromers at Tunstall, near the church. Work was started in the reign of King James I but the materials were not long afterwards purchased by Sir Robert Viner and used in the building of his house in Lombard Street in London, which later became the general post office. All that was left was the foundations and vaulted cellars which were afterwards known by the name of 'the ruins' and were for many years the rendezvous of thieves and beggars. They became such a nuisance to the neighbourhood that the vaults were blown up with gunpowder and otherwise destroyed "to prevent future resort to them".

Hudson's Bay cats roamed wild near Mereworth and the trick of sawing a man in half had already been launched hundreds of years before the modern conjurors in Penshurst church, the victim being Sir Stephen de Penchester, as you can see if you look at his tomb today. And in the reign of Edward I, Sir Roger de Leybourne slew one Ernulf de Mountenay "at a meeting of the Round Table held at Walden in Essex".

The coast of France, that dear land with chalk cliffs corresponding to those of Kent from which so many imported cultures have emanated, you can see on any reasonably clear day from points all the way from

County Hall, Maidstone

Broadstairs to Hythe. From the two Channel ports of Dover and Folkestone shuttle services ply to and from Zeebrugge, Ostend, Dunkirk, Calais and Boulogne; the streets of Dover, Canterbury and Folkestone resound in summer with French, German, Dutch and Italian, while the juggernaut lorries, coming from even further afield (the record so far is one from Afghanistan) make life

27

hideous and precarious on the main roads.

Chunnel? As a lover of Kent, I'll go through that tunnel when I come to it. If ever I do so it will be with the reflection that while the port of Dover will always be the gateway of England, Kent has now the tradesmen's entrance as well. I'm not sorry that it has been shelved.

There are towns in rural Kent, market towns, seaside resorts, and local centres. Before reorganization swept them all away, the county possessed a healthy array of municipal corporations, governing towns with, in at least one case (Canterbury), a history continuous from prehistoric times. Many of them were tiny and in fact, away from the Thames-side fringe and the 'Medway towns', the only centre with more than 50,000 inhabitants is the county town of Maidstone. Canterbury, the national shrine, and Dover, the busy port, though important and indeed pre-eminent in their own spheres, are much smaller. (When speaking of these towns we mean the old Canterbury and Dover and not the new 'districts' to which they have given their names.) Under 'reorganization' Deal and Sandwich now march under Dover's banner; Herne Bay and Whitstable under Canterbury's; while Folkestone is united with Hythe, Lydd and New Romney under the name, meant no doubt to be reminiscent of the Cinque Ports (or of the old lathe), of Shepway. The north coast has a string of smallish places, several of them masquerading under strange aliases as a result of these changes. Faversham and Sittingbourne are, with the Isle of Sheppey, swallowed nominally at least in the waters of a river. The Swale, the channel dividing the Isle of Sheppey from the mainland, once the name-giver for a rural area, now performs the same office for a much larger district, no longer 'rural'. The new name of Margate, Ramsgate and Broadstairs is attuned to history as well as geography. They were in origin mere sub-parishes of the parish of Minster, which shared the Isle of Thanet with its sister parish of Monkton. So these three towns are not inappropriately included in a district named Thanet.

Sevenoaks, Tonbridge and Ashford are other medium-sized places I have not mentioned; each fills its niche in the Kentish facade, while little Tenterden, with one foot in the Weald and the other in Romney Marsh, though coming last, would head the list for many people who value unassuming charm and unspoilt dignity; and Kent is fortunate in having so many of those places that can either be regarded as very small towns or very large villages – Lydd and New Romney, in spite of their former charters, Cranbrook, West Malling, Wye and Yalding, and even perhaps Wingham.

The little towns of Kent add further colour to the picture of a countryside already varied in its natural hues.

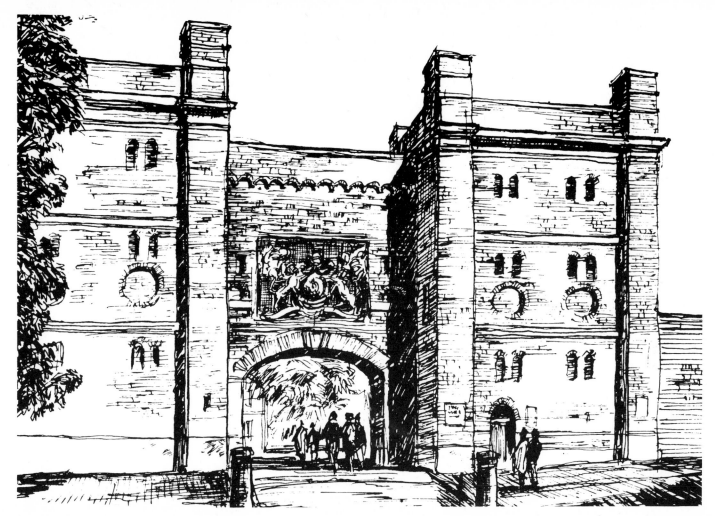

Chatham Dockyard, main gateway

CHAPTER TWO

"You Can't Live on Scenery"

Before we proceed to look at the road system, the railways, the ports, the industries and the agriculture of Kent, we should perhaps compare notes with William Lambarde, in whose steps we are, to some extent at least, trying to follow. Dear Lambarde is a pleasant fellow to read; he has a turn of phrase at times quite modern, setting his face against 'old wives' tales', telling us how William II had too many irons in the fire, and Edward IV made hay while the sun shone. I forget who it was who was 'as hot as toast', and who got himself into a hurly-burly. Lambarde certainly did touch on industry, and had quite a lot to say about agriculture; one is quite surprised at his depth of knowledge of the social, legal, and financial organization of the county; it is interesting to learn that "The gentlemen be not heere [throughout] of so auncient stockes as elsewhere, especially in the partes neerer to London, from whiche citie (as it were

from a certeine riche and wealthy seed plot) courtiers, lawyers, and marchants be continually translated, and do become new plants amongst them." He knew nothing of railways, naturally, and thought that lists of gentry and their parks and forests, of the payments of "tenths and fifteenths" set out parish by parish, of castles, beacons, fairs and franchises to be of interest, rather than roads and ports. Perhaps Lambarde was wise to stick to those subjects that he really knew about; to do full justice to the topics we have proposed would require a panel of expert writers. One can only hope to sketch in a background quite lightly, with perhaps a little more detail of the things that affect the country scene directly, or indirectly.

Beginning with the road system, although it is not too bad on the whole, it suffers because so much attention has to go to the London–continental link. Here you have two trunk routes, both starting in London and both ending at Dover. What we used to call the A2, but now the A2–M2, is to all intents and purposes the old Roman road from the capital through the cathedral towns, Rochester and Canterbury; however little history you may have remembered, those long straight lines on the map tell their own tale. The new motorway is quite sinuous by comparison: it leaves the old main road just before Rochester, crosses the Medway on a viaduct, curls

Viaduct over the Medway

Swanley and Wrotham Hill via Farningham, and then running south of them through Maidstone and Ashford to Folkestone, with an extension to Dover again, is a second trunk route, as many know, the A20. Before the Medway towns bypass was built – the M2 – most people in East Kent used to prefer this more southerly route – the A20 – for getting to town, although it meant considerable extra mileage, because of the restriction, congestion and chaos all through the coastal and Medway towns. Now of course they use the A2–M2 which is dual from the Rochester end of the motorway all the way to Eltham in the Greater London area.

But the coming of the M2 is only one episode in the long fight against congestion on the Kentish roads which goes on continuously. As soon as you deal with a problem you find that its nature changes, or another one altogether crops up. Canterbury, for example, is a nerve centre of the road system of East Kent, and has been for generations a bottleneck. The problem used to be that of the holiday traffic going from London to the Thanet towns. It is interesting today to read reports prepared soon after the last war which tell us that in those days the traffic from London to Dover through Canterbury was virtually negligible; so, at colossal expense, the Thanet traffic was diverted on to the coastal road, avoiding the city. This was fine, but no sooner had it been done than

away through the Downs and does not rejoin Watling Street till they meet at Brenley corner, seven miles short of Canterbury. So there you have about sixty miles of trunk route mopping up the cream of the money that the Government makes available for the Kent roads. But that is only half the tale. Crossing the Downs between the traffic in the Dover direction, encouraged by the construction of the M2, began to mount up alarmingly so that Canterbury again became a bottleneck. At more expense this new flood of vehicles was sluiced off on to a ring road. With what result? The Dartford Tunnel was opened, linking north-west Kent with Essex. This brought a vehicular flood from the Midlands and North on to the A2–M2, and to make matters worse at the other end of the road the continental container-lorries had discovered the Channel car-ferries. At times the congestion on Canterbury's dual carriageway is as great as when everything had to go over the sixteen-foot-wide medieval King's Bridge. I say "as great" but it is a great deal more terrifying, and I have no doubt that other Kent towns have suffered in the same way – Sandwich, for instance, Tonbridge, Ashford and Maidstone. I quote all this just as a sample of the perennial problems stemming from Kent's geography. The physical dangers of the Dover road are, we hope, temporary only. Outside the city the route is (1975) – apart from a few miles – still narrow and dangerous; people are being killed, and properties demolished by the heavy lorries from the Continent, and life made unendurable in what were once peaceful villages. Sit-downs on the road, noisy demonstrations and harrying of Members of Parliament are now regular features of existence in those places, and who can blame them. Let us hope that, by the time these words are read, all this will be in the past.

Another trouble-spot at the other end of the county was the London–Hastings road which caused fearsome traffic tangles in Sevenoaks and Tonbridge, which have now been bypassed at immense expense.

There is a pretty comprehensive network of roads linking Kent's many small and medium-sized towns, a network which is perhaps better than those in neighbouring counties, yet has some narrow and winding sections. The Ministry have an expression, I have heard, the "rural main road", which well describes these roads, pleasant enough for the weekend motorist who is not in any particular hurry, but scarcely up to European standards. Even a quite important link like the Thanet–Hastings road through Canterbury, the Stour Valley and Ashford has had virtually nothing done to improve it since I came to live in Kent.

The Weald had a tradition of bad roads. Conditions can still be pretty mucky when the water company or the electricity people have been laying their pipes and cables, or when one of our farmer friends has had his tractors working a field with a gate on to the highway; I believe the county council has several notice boards to warn the traffic – with three letters each about four feet high – M – U – D.

The Wealden mud finds its way into everything, even into these pages, not that things haven't improved greatly in the last couple of hundred years; obviously they must have.

By the way, one of Kent's most twisty, winding, frustrating roads is the one across Romney Marsh from Hythe to Rye. This is the road along the Rhee Wall. Friends who know about the history of the Marsh tell me that you could once see alongside the Rhee Wall the old course of the Rother when it used to empty into the sea at Romney. Whether this continued until modern times, or whether the road widening that is taking place has anything to do with its disappearance I don't know, but certain it is that I can't see the old course of the Rother now. Near Old Romney there is a sort of depression, but it seems to be on the wrong, i.e. north-eastern, side of the Wall.

Probably the most interesting road in Kent is the 'Pilgrims' Way', leading from Winchester to Canterbury and Dover, which I read is a prehistoric trackway and really nothing specifically to do with pilgrims at all. The Kent section is by no means continuous — I am speaking partly from personal knowledge and partly from the map — but it keeps on cropping up at intervals. Beginning at the Surrey border there is a short length between there and Chevening, then comes a gap of a mile or two before you pick it up again near Kemsing, whence is a run of several miles through Wrotham to Birling. You are now on the edge of the Medway valley which interrupts the road for some distance; there seems to be some difference of opinion as to which of the roads on the eastern side of the valley is or is not the Pilgrims' Way, but it starts up again for sure near Boxley, just north of Maidstone, and then follows a scenic course along the foot of the Downs escarpment, with magnificent views south to the greensand ridge, as far as Lenham. There it peters out; but it soon appears again at Hart Hill and carries on sometimes as a mere track, sometimes as a metalled road, nearly to Eastwell. We are now within a mile or two of the Stour valley, and from here on there are — or seem to the uninitiated to be — only disconnected small lengths of the Way until you arrive at the outskirts of Canterbury. But the narrow road that skirts Wye and Brabourne Downs is considered to be a second branch of the Pilgrims' Way , which is last seen on the Downs north of Folkestone heading towards Dover. The Canterbury–Dover section makes a good start and runs for several miles through the orchards to Patrixbourne and beyond, but finally gives up the ghost on the Downs between Adisham and Bishopsbourne. Its last problematic appearance is near the mining village of Tilmanstone, where it seems to be

33

heading in the wrong direction – for Kingsdown, near Deal, rather than for Dover.

In recent years has come the idea of long-distance footpaths, one of which is the North Downs Way. It starts and ends exactly as does the Pilgrims' Way, and might be confused with it; but the two coincide only here and there, apart from the stretch from Hollingbourne, near Maidstone, to Eastwell, near Ashford. Elsewhere, especially where the old road has been metalled, the footpath seems to run approximately parallel with it about three-quarters of a mile higher up the escarpment of the Downs. Anyone who has driven along the narrow made-up stretches of the Pilgrims' Road and has met the hurtling Land Rover of the nonchalant agriculturalist will understand the reason for this.

But the main roads and the Pilgrims' Way are only a small proportion of the whole. Kent has an unrivalled web of country roads and tiny lanes, some quite wide and comfortable winding their way through pleasant places tucked away in the fastnesses of the Downs or dreaming time away forgotten by most of the world in the remoter parts of the Weald; others leading by the back door to the end of nowhere, and heaven help you if you meet another car of any size and there isn't a passing place near at hand for one of you to reverse to.

A simple way to enjoy much of Kent without effort is to take a byroad occasionally. Going to and from Canterbury and Ramsgate, who ever travels through Monkton and Minster? Those who never do are missing something good. Even a pleasant road can have an equally pleasant alternative. The Charing–Pluckley–Biddenden route from East Kent to the Weald and Tonbridge is pretty, but it can be varied by a quieter diversion from Pluckley to Three Chimneys, running westward of Smarden and Biddenden. Again, part of the course of the main Maidstone–Canterbury road is from the top of Charing Hill to Chilham. It is no further in distance, though naturally the road is slower, to take the more peaceful alternative through Broomfield corner and Shottenden, joining up to the old Faversham–Chilham cross-country road. And how many people could find their way from Canterbury to Dover without touching the main A2 road? This is possible, through Bekesbourne, Adisham, Ratling, Barfreston, Eythorne, Waldershare and Whitfield. Those who live in West Kent will know of plenty of similar alternatives. The Maidstone–Yalding–Lamberhurst route to Sussex would be one example.

Then, Kent is a fine place for armchair travel with books and maps. Old houses or even simple farms are

Oast-houses

Stephenson's 'Invicta' locomotive in the Dane John, Canterbury

Next on my list are the railways, but we must not forget that before the railways came there was the era of the canals. I found out by accident that there was a canal from Higham to Frindsbury near Rochester (where the oil platforms are being manufactured). It went under the hill through a tunnel that was later taken over to be used for the railway. And the Medway, too, was canalized from Tonbridge to Rochester, and was used for the products of the ironworks of the Weald. I think we are apt to forget how important water transport was before the railway age; it was the only satisfactory means of carrying really heavy weights, and the most convenient, where it existed, for passengers. In 1842 when Canterbury Cricket Week started, the London contingent came by water to Margate and from thence by road, for though there were railways in Kent, there was not yet one linking Canterbury with London. I think we all know that Gravesend made a lot of money out of its monopoly of the ferry traffic between there and London.

It is strange that Canterbury was somewhat late in getting connected with London, because it had for some time before 1842 had its own little railway to Whitstable – one of the earliest passenger railways in the world, on which our famous Invicta locomotive used to ply. They still preserve this engine – outdoors if you please – in the Dane John Gardens at Canterbury; surely it should be

often there with the words 'manor' or 'court' added to remind us of the time when the holding of the old feudal courts brought a little grist to the squire's mill. This kind of homework will transform real and actual travel, revealing unsuspected things to look for and new facets of the old.

36

put under cover. I hear that it has been scheduled as an ancient monument; I should be interested to hear what the lawyers have to say about that. It seems to me that it is a movable thing – it has a few feet of line that it can run up and down if coaxed.

Another railway curiosity we have in the county is the smallest commercially operated railway in the world, the Romney, Hythe and Dymchurch, opened in 1927, fifteen-inch gauge, fourteen miles of track. It is really just a holiday attraction I suppose, but the level crossings over some of the Romney Marsh roads look rather dangerous to me. Some time ago there was a collision with a car and the train came off worst – yes, sad to relate, the engine-driver lost his life.

Having mentioned these few odd facts, what more can one say? We have complete electrification of course, and generally speaking the rail system is like the roads, with the London, Chatham, Canterbury and Dover line competing with one further south, with the difference that this latter one takes the route Sevenoaks, Tonbridge, Ashford, instead of Maidstone–Ashford, and the county town is not in fact on a main line. Another difference between rail and road is the greater importance to the former of commuters. When the north-east line divides at Faversham the extension to Thanet is regarded as the main line because of the large number of first-class season

Ashford-built locomotive used on the London-Dover line

ticket holders living there. There are not many commuters in Canterbury or Dover and this line is regarded as of little account compared with the Thanet one. Perhaps the new university at Canterbury will redress the balance a little.

When we talk about ports we must think, first and foremost, of Dover. It is now the busiest passenger harbour in the country, and the foremost roll-on roll-off port in the whole world. For fear that the name for this latter species of traffic should prove too much of a mouthful it has been shortened to RORO. No one who lives on the routes that lead to Dover, especially the A2, needs telling that its traffic has increased, but for those who want statistics, the number of cars going through (accompanied motor vehicles, as they are classified) rose to a peak in 1973 of well over a million, and by 1974 the total of lorries (outward and inward) had attained more than 250,000; in 1974 the total number of passengers approached six million. The causes of this phenomenal growth are obvious – continental travel is popular and the so-called juggernauts have arrived, the cross-Channel container-lorries sporting the TIR label. Folkestone also has been doing well and some of the traffic scared away from the union-dominated big ports has helped the development of the Medway harbours, and of Ramsgate, Richborough, near Sandwich, and even little Whitstable. All this is very different from the days when places like Romney and Sandwich were the cocks of the walk as Cinque Ports; one hates to see places with so much history fading out of the commercial picture, but that is life. And I don't forget that Dover is a Cinque Port.

To complete the picture of the county's communications we must surely mention airports and

Dover harbour

hoverports: Kent has everything. Every time we go to Ramsgate or Broadstairs from places west we pass the old Battle of Britain fighter station at Manston; it still has a role as a base for commercial hiring and charter flights. The highest spot in Thanet, it has some wonderful views: you can see the sea in two directions, and from the same spot Reculver towers and Bell Harry at Canterbury. I am told that when it is very clear the view extends to Essex, France, and the Stour valley up to Godmersham, but I cannot personally vouch for this.

In the period after the war great things were hoped for Lydd, from which holiday shuttle services were run. Then the so-called Ashford Airport at Lympne seemed to have taken over the running, but now Lydd has come back and Lympne is closing down. There is another airport at Rochester.

Hoverports are now, of course, the thing of the moment. There is one at Dover, next to the car-ferry terminal, run by the railways, and the private enterprise undertaking at Pegwell Bay. A little strange, isn't it, that at the place where the Saxons landed, and where later old St Augustine came ashore to teach us to be better boys, now there is little to see but a terminus for these strange machines that glide over land as if it were water, and would have frightened poor old Augustine, not to mention Hengist and Horsa, out of their wits.

Kent's 'dirty' industry (I believe in calling a spade a spade, and if anyone regards cement works as atmospherically 'clean' I am prepared to discuss the point) is concentrated, as one would expect, in the area along the Thames, which is fortunately outside my brief, and to a lesser extent, the Medway.

Visually, the electricity generating works at Northfleet have attracted what must be one of the most awe-inspiring wirescapes to be found anywhere in this country, and I am glad that I do not have to describe it — words would undoubtedly have failed me. The industrial landscape of Sittingbourne much farther east may be grim also, but the Bowater paper mills bring employment and prosperity.

We have already heard that Maidstone is an industrial town, and unfortunately for the beauty of the Medway valley the business community has set up, at various times, white-smoking cement works with their attendant gashes and scars in the downland between Maidstone and Rochester. This is not criticism — as a nation we have to live, and one can't live on scenery. An oil refinery is an oil refinery, and we have a big one at Grain, and now oil drilling platforms are being made at Frindsbury.

As small boys many of us held Maidstone in some esteem as the place where Sharp's Super Kreme Toffee was made; we no longer hear of this product, because a transfer to peppermints has put an end to the name. Meanwhile the county town seems to have overspilled, industrially, into Aylesford and New Hythe, which with Larkfield and Ditton have developed into a new complex, with the great Reed's paper works at its heart. The manufacture of paper (though not on the modern scale) at Aylesford is very ancient. I have already told of

39

A Kentish coal-mine

the contrast between the scene round the Friars and the bridge, and the nearby factories.

The kind of industry that one likes to see in a county like Kent is the specialist one having a bit of interest and character of its own, and neither noisy, overpowering in scale, nor belching forth fumes. I have in mind the making of the Dormobile at Folkestone, wooden houses

at Bethersden and plastic tiles at Marley, though tiles aren't made there any more — it's the foam rubber section.

In one corner of the North Downs is a small coalfield which once had four pits, but now only three (Snowdown, Tilmanstone and Betteshanger). The mines are deep and hot, and so are the miners' leaders; the field produces less coal and proportionately more noise than any other in the kingdom.

Most of us love the countryside and its pursuits, but only a farmer could do full justice to them. The agriculturalist these days has to be an expert who knows the ins and outs of government controls, subsidies and Common Market regulations amongst other things. At the same time, some of those old farmers are amazingly knowledgeable about the architecture, history and so forth of their own districts — you'd be surprised. A doctor friend of mine went to live in a most impressively ancient timbered building on the edge of the Weald, to the name of which he added the word 'manor'. One of our farmer friends, a man of the old school, sucking a straw, gumboots thick with manure, told him the house's history. Before being a 'manor' it had been called a plain 'house', and before that, when the farmer was a young lad, a 'cottage'. It had indeed come up in the world.

One hears things as one moves around. Hops are in

decline, and fashions in fruit fluctuate, sometimes leaving a farmer with whole orchards that have become a liability rather than an asset. The great days of hop-picking, when there was a mass invasion from the East End, are over. We now have machines that can do the work after a fashion, but lack of interest by the East-Enders has as much to do with it as mechanization. One result of the decline has been that large numbers of the oast houses have been converted into dwelling-houses, and very attractive ones they make. Another feature in decline (more's the pity) are the Romney Marsh sheep. There are still a lot of them, but we see field after field being taken away from grazing and used for growing corn, or even market-garden products. Fruit as a whole is as popular as ever, and new orchards are still being planted. The soft fruit growers nowadays counter the labour shortage by the pick-it-yourself system.

You have only to look around to see how prosperous our farmer friends are. They keep up-to-date with their mechanization, marketing schemes, silos, static fruit-spraying installations and anti-frost screens. As long as they are doing well not only do we get the food they produce but quite a lot of fun 'spins off' as they say today – hunting and point-to-point racing in their several seasons, and in the summer agricultural shows and gymkhanas.

Yes, agriculture is still Kent's economic mainstay, and it will be a sorry day for the county if ever it ceases to be so.

Nowadays 'industry' does not mean only what goes on in factories and workshops. Anything from insurance to race relations can be so described if you wish. There was a time when bribery and corruption might have been considered a minor industry in some places. Centuries ago, the monks of Faversham established something of a record by bribing *the king* with "two hundred marks in a purse and a fair Palfrey for his own sadle"; and at Queenborough the principal source of wealth was the election for members of parliament which secured for the chief inhabitants lucrative places in various branches of the government. Even the great Sir Roger Manwood, Queen Elizabeth's Chief Baron of the Exchequer, and an active philanthropist, was not above using his position to bend the law when it suited him.

Yet Kentish people generally, prided themselves on their honesty and considered that they suffered by returning the true value of their lands for tax purposes when "estates in the northern counties of this kingdom, whose inhabitants are noted for being wary, even to a proverb, are taxed at but an eighth, or a fourth part in proportion to this county ..."

One of Kent's most lucrative (and legitimate)

industries in the wider sense must be tourism in its various forms. It benefits all the coast east of the Medway round almost to Dungeness, particularly the Thanet towns. Inland, Canterbury is obviously pre-eminent with its 800 years of experience; the pilgrims that Chaucer described were the tourists of the Middle Ages, and the tourists of today often call themselves pilgrims. Dear old Canon Gostling, who died in 1777 and left behind him a book that has since gone through many editions, *A Walk in and about Canterbury*, mentions visitors from America even in his day. He vividly describes their reactions to the cathedral: "At the first entrance with such into this noble structure, how have I enjoyed their astonishment! How have I seen the countenances even of their negroes sparkle with raptures of pleasure and admiration! Raptures which no language but that of the eyes is capable of expressing."

Some years ago a government-sponsored 'Economic Planning Council' criticized Canterbury (goodness knows on what basis) for not doing enough to attract tourists. The tart reply of a city spokesman, that Canterbury had been drawing innumerable visitors centuries before anybody dreamed of setting up economic planning councils and would continue to do so long after they were forgotten, was pounced on gleefully by the international press and published as far away as East Africa. To be strictly truthful and objective, the name of Canterbury is far better known throughout the world than is that of the county of Kent. Nevertheless the shire as a whole is really one great attraction, with the tourists making for the sea and for villages, churches, country seats, ancient monuments, and places where great men have passed.

CHAPTER THREE

Commuter Coast

When you travel up and down the same railway line five days a week for eleven months of the year as the commuters do you don't really *see* anything of the country. When you glance out of the window – which isn't often – it is only to check where you are. A cow may look at your train as it passes but it hasn't the brain to comprehend what it is, and in the same way the people in the train may look at the fields and villages without knowing or caring enough to appreciate them.

It is certainly not for the scenery en route that people commute from a distance to Whitstable, Herne Bay, and especially Thanet. They suffer from the long journey, from overcrowded trains, from strikes and go-slows, from fares that go up at regular intervals. But most of them in that part of the world think that the joy of the sea air after a day in the City makes it all worth while. And the hours in the train enable a man to catch up on his work without interruption, read the newspaper thoroughly, or even enjoy an illegal game of solo, if so minded.

Two books reissued a short time ago recommend a rail trip as a good introduction to the parts of Kent they describe, the Weald and Romney Marsh. It is a sign of the times that both lines are now closed except for the partial use of one of them, by railway enthusiasts, as a museum piece. Yet the North Kent line, beloved of the commuter, stays open; even the good Dr Beeching did not propose to close a railway that must be one of BR's best money-spinners. As a scenic route however it leaves much to be desired, to say the least. On the down line, as soon as you leave Greater London you are in Swanley – more built up than the London green belt through which you have just come. Then you plunge into a series of cuttings and emerge only to cross the ugliest bit of the Darent valley on a high viaduct. There are bits of open country round the suburban settlements of Longfield and Meopham, but cuttings soon swallow you again. As the train gathers impetus down the long incline to the Medway you have a glimpse of some charming hill-and-dale country near Cobham (itself quite invisible from the train) but almost immediately you are passing the back gardens of the little villas on the outskirts of Strood. The line curves in such a way that you see not only the cathedral but also all four sides of the keep of Rochester Castle, as well as views over the industrialized reaches of the River Medway and of the motorway viaduct over it. Grain and Sheppey flit by in the distance, but generally, the Medway landscape is grimy and depressing as seen from the train, a vista of broken concrete, abandoned bits of railway, over-full scrapyards, slatey, obsolete houses and grim Victorian stations, just tarted up enough to make the older parts look worse than ever. Beyond Gillingham, you find Rainham, Sittingbourne and Teynham are just as depressing and Faversham not much less so. Admittedly there is charming orchard country in between, and the view once a year of Newington church seen across a great sea of apple blossom is a classic one, that used to be a favourite of *The Times.* Beyond Faversham there are coastal marshes, Graveney church, the estuary and townscape, with sea glimpses all the way from Seasalter to Beltinge; then more marshes and you are in Thanet. This is the island so many of the commuters make such sacrifices to live in.

It is easy to make fun of the Isle of Thanet. To begin with it isn't an island at all, any more than several other 'isles' in our county – Oxney, Grain and Elmley, to name a few. Then, for the scoffers, the vogue of the jellied eel, bottled beer and whelks, of funfairs, bingo and the dog-track, confined though it may be to certain limited areas of the seaside, gives a ready-made opportunity for wit.

In fact, however, if you take the entire area of the three Thanet resorts, Margate, Broadstairs and Ramsgate, with all their hotels and boarding houses, their shopping and business zones and the old and new residential areas where the commuters, retired people and ordinary residents live, it amounts to well under half the area of the island, perhaps about two-fifths. The rest is open country.

As most people know, Thanet was an actual island in Roman times and the ships going to and from London used not to go round the treacherous North Foreland, but took the short cut through the strait known as the River Wantsum that separated Thanet from the mainland, with the twin fortresses of Richborough and Reculver guarding its two mouths. The most important communication with the island was the ferry at Sarre, now a busy road junction. The Wantsum ceased to be anything but a tiny stream about the time of Henry VII. There is a very well-known quotation from John Twyne, Mayor of Canterbury and first Headmaster of the King's School there, who died in Queen Elizabeth's reign: "There be right credible persons yet living that have often seene, not only small boates, but vessels of good burden, to passe to and fro, upon this Wantsume, where now the water (especially towards the West) is cleane excluded."

Now, the once celebrated River Wantsum is represented at its northern end by an iron pipe in which a trickle flows or is arrested at the whim of the Southern Water Authority. Eastwards from a point near Sarre, the old Wantsum is more worthily represented by the lower reaches of the River Stour, making its way from its old mouth to join the sea at Pegwell Bay.

Before the craze first for sea bathing and later for mass seaside holidaymaking, the island was a sort of horticultural Garden of Eden. It was described in the late eighteenth century as follows:

> … by the excellent husbandry of the landholders, who are noted for it to a proverb in these parts, the crops of corn are abundantly large, and Thanet wheat and barley, for its cleanliness and weight, fetch a superior price at markets of all others. Canary-seed is likewise produced on the lands here in great quantities, as well as the seeds of radish, spinach, mustard, cabbage, and other esculent plants, which are sent from hence for the supply of the London markets; in short, the high state of cultivation throughout the island gives an idea rather of the delicate work of a gardener, than the effect of the more enlarged industry of the husbandman. The farms throughout the island are mostly large and considerable, and the farmers wealthy, insomuch that they are usually denominated gentlemen farmers on that account, as well as from their hospitable and substantial mode of living.

Margate, street scene

Thanet is still a market garden on a huge scale, with vast fields of onions, broccoli, and other vegetables. Until the eighteenth century, Margate was rated as "a poor inconsiderable fishing town". But:

> From this state of insignificance Margate rose unexpectedly … to wealth and consequence, owing principally to the universal

recommendation of sea air and bathing, and the rage of the Londoners at the same time of spending their summer months at those watering places situated on the sea coast; and when it came to be known that the shore here was so well adapted to bathing, being an entire level and covered with the finest sand, which extends for several miles on each side the harbour, and the easy distance from the metropolis, with the conveniency of so frequent a passage by water, it gave Margate a preference before all others, to which the beauty and healthiness of it, and of the adjoining country, contributed still more.

In these early times, Thanet's climate was compared favourably with that of towns on the Channel coast: " ... those grateful gales, which produce fine warm weather and render the Margate shore smooth and pleasant, never fail to occasion at the same time a continual swell and surf of the sea on the south coast of England; which not only makes the water there foul and thick, but annoys, spatters, and frightens the bathers exceedingly." So much for Brighton and Eastbourne.

One hesitates to impose on the reader more highly improving quotations, about the invention of the bathing machine by Mr Beale, the Quaker.

Those who think of Margate sands as being practically invisible under the mass of trippers at holiday times may at first be surprised to know that the writer has been on the sands near the Foreshore in August bank holiday when there was not another solitary soul in sight. This was during the war, when the town was a 'defence area' and there actually was grass growing in streets where today the holiday-makers throng. The idea of precaution against invasion was nothing new. The eighteenth-century author already quoted mentions that to the west of Margate the inhabitants had cut several hollow ways through the cliffs to give access to the sea; "but they have been frequently forced to fill them up again in time of war, to prevent their being made use of by the enemy, to surprize and plunder the country".

With seaside and bathing on our minds we may not think of the Margate suburb of Birchington as a place steeped in history, though the tomb of Dante Gabriel Rossetti in the churchyard is well known. The nearby park of Quex recalls the medieval family of Quek or Queake. An early nineteenth-century mansion has replaced the ancient house, and the Waterloo tower, a tall monument with a spire made of cast iron, dates itself. After the Queks came the Crispes and one of these, Henry, was involved in an incident quite reminiscent of modern hijackings and kidnappings.

In the Middle Ages one of the war aims of any doughty warrior was to hit the jackpot by capturing a wealthy man who could be held to ransom. This barbarous practice has become commonplace in our

St George's Church, Ramsgate

kidnapped poor Mr Crispe, whisked him off to Bruges in Flanders and then demanded a ransom of £3,000 for his release. The family were trying to scrape the money together when Oliver Cromwell got wind of the transaction and promptly vetoed it as a royalist plot to export money illegally for the support of their king. After a long delay, permission was given for the ransom to be paid and Mr Crispe returned to England. *Bonjour* was the only French his captors could get out of him, even after several months, and Bonjour Crispe he was called from that time onward.

Margate's rival resort, Ramsgate, has an amusement area called, incongruously one would have thought, 'Merrie England' (Margate's is 'Dreamland'). Ramsgate's visitors, too, or some of them, have a taste for shellfish and ale, or candyfloss and ice-cream according to their ages, but life here centres much more round the harbour, which is on a different scale altogether from Margate's Rennie-designed but tiny haven.

Until the eighteenth century the harbour was only a bit of a wooden jetty, as Leland saw on his Perambulations: "Ramsgate a 111j myles upward in Thanet, wher as is a smaul peere for shyppeis." The village was a limb of the Cinque Port of Sandwich, to which it definitely had to play second fiddle. It was to the merchants of the City of London that Ramsgate

modern decadence, but in the seventeenth century would still cause some eyebrows to be raised, as happened in the case of Bonjour Crispe. The time was that of the Commonwealth, when Charles II was conducting his government in exile. At dead of night the terrorists, as they would now be termed, Englishmen and others, owed its rise: when Sandwich was petitioning for money to try and revive its harbour, the London people made a counter petition, saying that the money would be better spent on improving Ramsgate. Nothing was done, until one day there was a terrible storm and many of the passing ships had to take refuge in Ramsgate's little harbour. The Government then woke up to the urgency of the problem and agreed to a large stone-built harbour being made at Ramsgate. The loud clamours of Sandwich at this example of the tail wagging the dog were met by the grant of a couple of hundred pounds a year out of Ramsgate's revenues to support Sandwich's harbour. But Ramsgate still had problems. Because their harbour was entirely artificial, and not based on a river mouth, there was no flow of water to clean it out, and it began to silt up as badly as poor old Sandwich's had done. In this difficult pass, Ramsgate had the good sense to call in a Yorkshireman, the engineer Smeaton. He told them to make an artificial cleaning-out current by creating a large basin where the water was stored at high tide, then after the tide had receded, the sluices were opened. When this had been done the waters gushed out into Pegwell Bay with such force that the harbour was cleaned out, mud, sand and the lot, down to the underlying chalk, and Ramsgate harbour has never looked back since.

Broadstairs

The western cliffs of Ramsgate overlook Pegwell Bay, which always gives me the feeling that ghosts are brooding over it, perhaps because two of the greatest events in our history happened here, the landing of the Saxons and later of St Augustine. Yet there is little to show for them, only an insignificant stone column, a golf

48

course called 'St Augustine's', and the relic of a modern publicity stunt, the 'Viking Ship' that the Danes rowed across the North Sea in 1949. Even the racket of the hovercraft cannot dispel the mournful feeling that the nation cares little about any aspect of its history not concerned with battles, murders and sudden death.

Broadstairs has, its inhabitants consider, more charm than its neighbours, though concrete cliff works, necessary because of erosion, have lessened it. It remains a real kid's bucket-and-spade place in summer, and quiet and peaceful in winter; and with Kingsgate, St Peter's and the North Foreland it has quite a lot of things that, if not centuries and centuries old, have their little histories. The very name *Kings*gate is said to commemorate a landing there by Charles II and the Duke of York in 1683; the North Foreland lighthouse is the last of a distinguished line of predecessors using a varied assortment of lights from coal braziers to the present multi-candleflower beam; and nearby is the eighteenth-century seat Stone House. Hereabouts too, in the same century, Lord Holland, the father of Charles James Fox, built a grandiose folly, a huge house allegedly on the designs of Cicero's villa at Baiae. The grounds were stuffed with fake and genuine antiquities to such an extent that even eighteenth-century taste confessed itself disgusted. Apart from a much altered house and a few

Dent-de Lion gatehouse, Garlinge, Thanet

fragments adapted for humble use, all of this over-magnificent pile has disappeared. Though Broadstairs may have its little side-shows and Margate perhaps more important ones — the gateway of the Elizabethan house of the Dandelions (or Dent-de-Lions), the remains of Salmestone, the once magnificent grange of St

49

Augustine's abbey, and the still thriving Drapers or Yoakley's Hospital founded in 1709 – it is at the villages of Monkton and Minster in the southern part of the island that we find the starting points of fourteen centuries of Thanet history. The western half of the island comprised the manor of Monkton, given in AD 961 by Queen Ediva to the monastery of Christchurch in Canterbury, the present cathedral. Today Monkton has not slid so completely into the status of a suburb of the coastal towns as has its sister place of Minster, but remains basically a village, and a small, gaunt, straggly village at that. The church of rendered flint, very old though it is (twelfth century), looks forlorn; on my last visit it was locked, and typically, all the nearby cottages were deserted. If I were to say that there is not a great deal to see inside it will sound like 'sour grapes'.

About a mile away on the crest of the down is St Nicholas-at-Wade whose lofty church tower is a landmark for miles around. The fine castellated tower gives dignity to a peaceful backwater, where the residents take some pains to maintain what is old and to restrain what is new.

The story of Minster, and of the *eastern* half of Thanet, begins way back in AD 670 when King Egbert, misled by the bad advice of a courtier, Thunnor, had two of his

Minster Abbey, Thanet

cousins murdered, and in repentance granted half of the Isle of Thanet to their sister Domneva to found and endow a 'minster' or monastery for nuns. Thunnor came to a deservedly unpleasant end, being swallowed up by the ground while trying craftily to cut down the amount of land to be given to Domneva. The wicked courtier

50

tried to restrict the wanderings of a deer whose heavenly directed course was to delineate the boundaries of the gift. The Danes finally wiped out the monastery in 978, but it was a more civilized representative of their race, King Canute, who in the eleventh century gave the site of the old nunnery and the manor which endowed it – virtually the eastern half of Thanet – to St Augustine's Abbey, Canterbury.

Minster's modern expansion gives, at first, a misleading impression as one sees the villas strung out along the Monkton and Acol roads, the laundry and the old workhouse. But down the hill is more space, quiet and dignity. The church is one of the finest and most historic in Kent, its churchyard spacious and well trimmed; old buildings surround it at a respectful distance. The transepts, nave and aisles of St Mary's are a splendid piece of Norman work, the chancel is a little later, and at the western end are traces of the earlier Saxon building. The church is of impressive size, and the large transepts give it the ground plan of a cross, a fact that seems to have escaped the notice of the fanatic Richard Culmer in 1647. It was during the Civil War that this Puritan extremist, notorious as the man who smashed many of the stained glass windows in Canterbury cathedral, obtained, through sequestration, the care of Minster church. He observed that, on the spire, there was a globe and over that a large wooden cross covered with lead, and above it an iron cross. Regarding these as monuments of superstition, Culmer hired men to climb up the spire by moonlight and remove the crosses. Of this exploit Hasted remarks: "But if all the figures of a cross are monuments of idolatory and to be removed, the poor caitiff has done his work but by halves or rather not at all when he took down these from the spire and left the church standing, which is itself built in the form of a cross."

Only a stone's throw away, on a corner of the road, a high brick wall marks the curtilage of Minster Abbey. There are now two Minster Abbeys in Kent, since the church of Minster-in-Sheppey is also thus named. The Thanet one began its life as the court-lodge of the manor of Minster built by the monks of St Augustine's on the site that Canute gave them. It is a fine stone-built building, the main part being of Norman architecture, and the projecting wing possibly of Saxon. Such, at any rate, is the opinion of the present occupants, a chapter of Benedictine nuns who came to Minster in the 1930s. After the dissolution of the monasteries Minster Court, as it was then called, remained in private hands until the nuns bought it; they had fled from Bavaria to escape Hitler's persecution. After they had signed the contract to buy the house, Hitler confiscated the money they had

51

earmarked for the purchase; but American Benedictines came to the rescue. When the monks of old used the house as a grange for their Thanet farms they built a church there, and the remains of its tower can still be seen.

These, then, are just a few reminders of Thanet's historic past. One could tell of many more, for its countryside is dotted with farms and great houses that were in former time the manors and seats of the notable families, whose histories provide a virtually inexhaustible fount of stories.

The simile of the cow looking at the train was put into less forceful but perhaps more elegant words by old Canon Gostling, who in the eighteenth century wrote that classic book about Canterbury's antiquities. "It is one thing to see, and another to observe," said Canon Gostling.

There is much of interest along the northern coast of Kent that our commuter friends cannot see from the train; other things that they have perhaps merely not observed. Bayford Court, for instance, near Sittingbourne. Although it is nothing special to look at, its name figures prominently in history, in the fights between Alfred the Great and the Danes, and later between Earl Godwin and Edward the Confessor. More

excusably, they can neither see nor observe Cooling Castle, though they can indeed see the Hoo peninsula on which it stands. Nor is Minster-in-Sheppey visible, only the isle itself as a land mass.

Cooling's great moment in history came in the days of Sir Thomas Wyatt's rebellion against Mary Tudor. The rebels besieged it, and Sir John Cobham, who defended, was just about licked when the rebels tired of the fight and marched away. On the same peninsula, All Hallows is about the nearest you can get to the skyscrapers of Southend-on-Sea. They are about four miles away and look nearer, yet one can scarcely descry the longest pier in England jutting out towards Kent, so puny are most of the works of man.

Some people might say that to view Sheppey from a distance as a land mass was probably the best view you could get of it: distance in fact would lend enchantment. But they would be wrong, for there is much to see. Admittedly the approach to it from Key Street on the A2 road can only be described as miserable, except for the attractive village and church of Bobbing. The heart sinks, but the broad, well-surfaced road and massive, expensive lift-bridge over the Swale seem designed to boost the morale of Queenborough, Sheerness, and the small villages of the island.

Poor Queenborough! When they abolished it recently

Cooling Castle, captured according to some accounts by the rebel Sir Thomas Wyatt

its corporation was not losing as much history as some Kentish boroughs; it dated only from the time of Edward III. And centuries ago it lost the castle which was its *raison d'être*, Cromwell having ordered it to be raised to the ground. Its church has a roof painted by a Dutch artist, the gravestone of a whaling skipper showing his harpoon, and a relief of the lost castle, but all around are unlovely factories and grim streets.

At the top of a steep hill you will find the *other* Minster Abbey; it has a story of abbesses, Danes and Saxon kings, not unlike that of the Thanet Minster. But there are two buildings left to the nunnery founded in the seventh century, the fine, square, stone-built entrance gateway to the west of the present church, and that church's north aisle, which was the monastic chapel, the nave being the parish church. There are two well-known tombs, those of the Earl of Clarence, brother of Richard III, of malmsey-butt fame (alternatively it may be that of a governor of Queenborough Castle). The monument is covered with people's initials, most of them centuries old; so is the other outstanding tomb, much older (1300), that of Sir Robert Shurland. Various gory legends account for the horse's head which forms part of the decoration of the tomb. One version is that a soothsayer foretold that his horse would kill Sir Robert, so he promptly had its head cut off and got another mount. Later, when he was riding his new horse,

it threw him off and his head landed on the skull of the deceased animal, killing him. When fighting against soothsayers Sir Robert, like Julius Caesar before him, found that you just cannot win!

Our technical guide tells us of a highly remarkable twelfth-century column figure of the Virgin and Child under a canopy. Regrettably this information is out of date. The piece is now in the Victoria and Albert Museum — purchased by them from the church for £10,000.

The most moving experience of Sheppey is yet to come. Having glanced at Shurland near Eastchurch where Sir Robert dwelt and seen the long abandoned ruin of its Elizabethan mansion, and penetrated, as it seems, the ultimate fastnesses of Sheppey, one sees a fingerpost reading "Harty *4 miles*". The amount of space on the island is surprising.

The church, for there is no village, is on the so-called Isle of Harty, which a narrow ditch separates from the rest of Sheppey. Overlooking the Swale, it is set back from the road which has led through a farmyard, and stands in an expanse of greensward with few gravestones. It is a pleasant surprise to find it unlocked, and a greater one to find evidence of regular use and affectionate care, beyond what is found in some village churches, cleanliness, fresh flowers and a well filled visitors' book.

Harty church

In the lady chapel is a very well-known wooden chest .with a design in relief of two knights jousting. The landscape of Harty is mournful; huge flocks of birds sometimes wheel away as you approach, startled no doubt at human intrusion into their solitude.

Apologetic to the birds, but grateful to Sheppey, we return to the mainland with the feeling that even the less promising parts of Kent have their treasures if only you look for them.

Faversham is the last example of things seen but not observed by travellers eager only to be back in their beloved Thanet. It is a half-and-half place, with on the one hand hideous brewery, gas-works, creek with timber-yards, retorts and oil-tanks; on the other a delightful town hall on stilts, many old houses, of the sixteenth, seventeenth and eighteenth centuries, and above all Abbey Street. This, a show piece of genuine restoration, has pre-nineteenth century houses and at the far end a couple much older and half-timbered, one of which is Arden's House. Thomas Arden was murdered here by his wife, thus providing the plot for the sub-Shakespearean tragedy *Arden of Faversham*. A modern tragedy is that after all the affectionate care taken over the restoration of the old Abbey Street the result is largely spoilt by its being used as a free car park on both sides. The church has a different but equally sad story: it has interesting brasses and wall-paintings, but is a victim of over-restoration.

Faversham Market Place

CHAPTER FOUR

Cinque, Quatre, Trois ...

Personally I have nothing against the Cinque Ports, nothing at all — that would be a terrible thing to say! But, when it comes to old things, I like forts and castles and similar tangible reminders of the past rather than just ceremonial, which is about all that the Cinque Ports, as such, now have. Up to about 1400, the Confederation of the Cinque Ports was very powerful; it ceased to be so, but for about another 600 years managed to hang on to its legal privileges. These have now disappeared, and only the trappings remain, such as rights at the Coronation and fancy robes. The best of luck to them!

But give me a good solid fortress, Richborough Castle for instance. Just look at those gigantic ruins of a Saxon shore fort, a base for Roman troops protecting the coast — the Saxon shore — against the ravages of pirates — our ancestors. It is a rectangular fortress with walls still standing twenty feet high and thirteen feet thick, and enclosing a huge area, originally five acres. One corner has been lost because of landslips. But the Romans had been at Rutupiae (the Latin name) long before the shore fort was built in the third century. It was here that their invasion army landed in AD 43 under Aulus Plautius, the general of the Emperor Claudius. You can see the double ditch of their first camp. Hundreds of thousands of ancient coins have been dug up in the excavations. There is no village of Richborough, only a farm, but the name has been revived in modern times and applied to a military cross-Channel port in the Great War, to a large industrial estate, and to a power station built since World War II.

The new Richborough is just across the River Stour from Sandwich. This little town has had its day as a port — as one of our Kentish historians rather unkindly put it (I couldn't help noting the words): "it has descended to the same obscurity as other country towns." The Sandwichmen would hotly dispute this today, pointing out that they are the only town in Kent scheduled for preservation — let Canterbury put that in its pipe and smoke it — and that they are overrun with visitors in summer. Some old customs are kept at public demand, even though they may not serve any practical need, such as the sounding of the curfew at eight o'clock every evening from the tower of St Peter's church. They still celebrate the anniversary of St Bartholomew's Day in 1217, when they helped to defeat the French in a great sea battle. In its heyday, Sandwich, as one of the original Cinque Ports, supplied fifteen sail of armed ships for His Majesty before he had a Royal Navy to call on. For its pains Sandwich was repeatedly plundered and burnt by our cross-Channel neighbours, who were the King's usual opponents, but this was perhaps an occupational risk attached to a Cinque Port. It was a little hard, however, when it had similar treatment from Richard Nevill, Earl of Warwick (the Kingmaker), during the Wars of the Roses; descendants of his family at Birling must feel thoroughly ashamed of him. However, Sandwich managed to recover every time from these temporary misfortunes as long as the harbour continued to bring prosperity. But as progress brought larger ships for trading and for fighting, the haven which, if Sandwich was going to survive, should have been enlarged began instead to silt up. To make matters worse, the Pope of the time, who seems to have had ship-owning interests besides his ecclesiastical ones, let one of his great cargo ships get stuck in the Sandwich mud, which blocked the harbour up indefinitely. The other Cinque Ports were having similar difficulties, and it was not surprising that the kings of England decided to go in for a standing navy in preference for the somewhat hit-and-mass contractual arrangements with Sandwich, Romney, Hythe and the rest. After the fourteenth century these ports never enjoyed their old prosperity and position. For some reason, however, they managed (as I have said) to hold on to some of their old privileges, particularly legal and ceremonial ones, the two spheres, perhaps, in which the English tendency to conservatism is strongest.

In the reign of Queen Elizabeth, Sandwich in its decline received a shot in the arm from a settlement of Flemings who not only set up the manufacture of "sayes, baize and flannel" but also went in for horticulture — a trade not hitherto seen on a commercial scale in England — including the production of a specially esteemed sort of carrot.

Sandwich certainly did not go down without a fight and even as late as the eighteenth century was toying with a very radical scheme to make a new outlet to the sea towards Sandown to its south. But the government of the day could not afford the cost, and, when the central finances had looked up a little, preferred, as you have already been told, to put its money on Ramsgate. This was a very unkind cut. Sandwich might well have exclaimed "Et tu, Ramsgate; then perish Sandwich," because the Thanet village — that was all it was in those days — was what was called a 'limb' of the Cinque Port

Sandwich, Barbican and bridge

of Sandwich, a sort of subordinate jurisdiction, subject to its superior's magistrates.

You can quite understand why Sandwich is scheduled for preservation *as a town*: it is the place as a whole that is interesting rather than the individual buildings. The old part of Sandwich is much smaller than the old part of Canterbury, but in it the proportion of ancient buildings is probably higher. The Barbican, the Fishergate, St Bartholomew's Hospital, the Old Customs House, the Pilgrims, the Dutch House, the Old Manwood School, the King's House, are the sort of buildings that Sandwich people may quote at you if you ask them to be specific.

Of the Earls of Sandwich, the only one of whom history has anything good to say was the first, who, after being on the parliamentary side in the Civil War, eventually helped with the restoration of Charles II. He fought as an admiral against the Dutch, and was killed in action. The worst one was the fourth Earl who was first lord of the Admiralty in 1748 and from 1771 to 1782; he did more than any other single human being (not excluding George Washington) to ensure that America won the War of Independence. The ships that were sent out were in rotten condition (apart from there not being enough of them), the rigging was second-hand, and, on occasion, the bottom would fall out. The fighting admirals had to improvise, using supply vessels as

battleships and so forth. But again good, of a sort, came out of evil: this precious rascal, in order to keep body and soul together on his all-night gambling sessions, put a piece of meat between two slices of bread, and as a result the name of Sandwich is known throughout the whole civilized world.

Just near Betteshanger, by the way, and not far from the village of Ham, there is a signpost apparently pointing the way to Ham Sandwich.

Sandwich is a little more prosperous these days. It has a modest function as a shopping centre, and along the Ramsgate road to the north a considerable industrial estate has grown up and has prospered and has attracted amongst others a well-known foreign chemical manufacturing company. Reflected glory and some more material benefit have accrued from the two famous golf links, Royal St George's and Prince's down by the seashore of Sandwich Bay. At the first-mentioned course the official existence of women is denied: they may indeed play but have no standing, and must immediately let through any Lords of Creation who may be playing behind them. What is Women's Lib doing about this, one wonders.

To sailors Deal is significant as being the nearest land to the Goodwins. These sands, which so often figure in the

60

headlines as 'the treacherous Goodwins', 'Graveyard of shipping', and so forth, lie between the North and South Forelands about three miles offshore. They are twelve miles long and about five miles across at their widest part, although constantly shifting. At high water they are completely covered, but on the ebb they dry out for about a tenth of the whole area. There are three Trinity House light vessels, the North, East and South Goodwin, and together with a big collection of flashing buoys they make the nightscape of Deal a nocturne of winking and scintillating lights. Even with radar and other scientific aids the Sands still have plenty of 'customers', two of the star turns being a couple of American cargo vessels wrecked during 1946 and always visible. When the tide goes down you can see still more wrecks, and the Deal lifeboatmen have to be on their toes the whole time. The sand, according to a Kent historian, "consists of a more soft, fluid, porous, spongeous and yet withal tenacious matter than the neighbouring sands, and consequently is of a more voracious and ingurgitating property; so that should a ship of the largest size strike on it, in a few days it would be so wholly swallowed up by these quicksands that no part of it would be left to be seen." Something of an exaggeration today, as we have heard. The sands did, however, give protection from the easterly gales to the Downs, the channel and anchorage between the

Goodwins and the coast, and in the days of sail hundreds of ships would be anchored in the Downs waiting for a fair wind, and Deal became an important provisioning depot.

Wreck-spotting is one of the stand-by seafront amusements of the town, and the sea-fishing is pretty good too; middle-aged gentlemen can be seen staggering proudly up the beach bearing codfish half as big as themselves.

This steep shingle bank is, by common repute, the place where Julius Caesar landed on his two incursions into Britain, in 55 and 54 BC. Were these successful punitive expeditions as Caesar (who acted as his own war correspondent) claimed, or were they humiliatingly unsuccessful attempts to conquer Britain?

The modern fishermen have motorized winches on which they coil the steel hawsers that haul their vessels well above the high water mark for safety. Caesar had no such winches, and his fleet was damaged by gales, a fact that was probably decisive in forcing him to retire to Gaul. Not for the first time, or the last time in history, failure to master the sea was fatal to the aspiration of a land power. But for this there was probably nothing to prevent Caesar conquering the whole of Britain.

So Deal is on the invasion coast, and has three Tudor castles as a consequence – its own, the ruins at Sandown, and the headquarters of the Lord Warden of the Cinque

61

Ports at Walmer. All three were built as stark low-profile artillery nests. Of the three, Sandown has nearly all been washed away and Walmer has had the Lord Warden's ceremonial quarters built on to it, and is landscaped with ornamental gardens and so is less austere, more charming. Deal Castle, the centre of the three, grim compared with Walmer, is nearer to its original state but the ornamental castellation is an addition, and the design seems much more elaborate than that, described in historical accounts and depicted in old prints, of Henry VIII's castle. The central keep remains, but instead of the original four 'lunettes' we now have six semi-circular bastions one step lower, with an outer ring of six much larger bastions lower still, separated from the keep by a sort of passage-way. Then comes a dry moat and a curtain wall in the form of a series of gentle curves corresponding with the bastions. Inside, the whole fortress is honeycombed with passages and staircases amounting virtually to a maze, and an excellent place for family hide-and-seek, intentional or accidental. Until he has mastered the complex plan the unwary visitor seeking the way out may end up in the unscalable moat, or wishing to gain the roof may find himself out in the street. In the eighteenth century the keep was described as being "bomb proof".

After the peace of Sandwich, Deal seems a live,

Deal seafront

bustling place. From the old days when the town prospered from the shipping in the Downs, the sea-front has inherited an eighteenth-century seafaring sort of a look, quietly pleasant, though in fact this part of Deal dates mostly from the end of the seventeenth century; the town, although it is out-of-the-way, seems to have a kind of warm active life of its own. Perhaps the Royal Marines with their depot – and their band – give it the inspiration that a town needs, through the vigorous though indirect influence of salt water.

If we follow the coast to Dover we pass amongst other places St Margaret's Bay. A few houses, a promenade and a car park, nestling against the South Foreland at the bottom of a steep hill with alpine hairpin bends, replace the exclusive hide-outs of pre-war. Dual use as commando training ground for our men and practice target for German gunners at Sangatte finished the old St Margaret's Bay, but not its importance as the place where the continental telecommunication cables come ashore. Up the hill, St Margaret's-at-Cliffe has a large and impressive Norman church. Extra windows in the chancel, and the tower with its arch, are the only modifications of the original design.

To hundreds of people who follow the sea, Dover means work; it is the port they sail from on the cross-Channel run. Those who use the port to earn their daily bread are inclined to take its history for granted, and in any case, Dover's history is still being made: we have already heard the statistics of the business it is doing. The castle, up on the eastern heights and continuously garrisoned from the time when Henry II built it to a few years ago, is a picturesque enough background for the port and harbour, and a good seamark. For those who are interested in medieval fortifications, armour and old weapons, and do not mind climbing endless steps so long as there is a good view at the top, it is a good place for an afternoon visit. In the reign of King John, Dover Castle was the key to the strategic situation when the Dauphin of France invaded England in support of the barons who were in open rebellion, and Hubert de Burgh successfully defended it in the King's cause. John was very fond of Kent and often visited it; perhaps he was not as black as history has painted him.

Inside the castle walls the great attraction is the Norman keep that towers over them. Not so much attention is paid to St Mary's church, although it is much older, a Saxon building. Dovorians tell me that until the middle of the last century it was nothing but a ruin, a shell. Our energetic Victorian ancestors restored it, and it requires an expert to point out which parts are original and which the Victorian work. Of more interest to me is the Roman pharos or lighthouse that stands next to the church; the Romans built this in the first century, as they did the companion pharos (now destroyed) on the western heights. It is thought that they were about eighty feet high and guided the cross-Channel shipping from Boulogne to Dover. I like to think of the Roman skippers ordering their helmsmen to steer towards the same mark that the Sealink and Townsend-Thoresen

Dover, St Mary-in-the-Castle and the Roman lighthouse

crews can see today.

crews can see today.

The white cliffs, even after many years of seeing them loom out of the mist and disappear into the rain-squalls, as well as soaking up the summer sun, can still give one a sort of pang of sentiment, off-white though they may be from close at hand and pitted with man-made embrasures serving various highly mysterious purposes.

But, more important, Dover is a great harbour. Perhaps in the dog-days on the lowest ebb it may come over a little somnolent, but most of the time there is movement, activity, something to see. That's what I like about Dover.

The boys at Dover College assemble in the old refectory of St Martin's Priory; until the Reformation it was the home of Benedictine monks. It is easy to remember which archbishop founded this priory: it was Corbeuil, sometimes spelt Carboil. It is the Carboil touch that fixes the name in the memory of any motorist to whom the problems of overheating are not unknown. Old Carboil was the next-but-one primate before Becket.

It is now time to up anchor, cast off, and steer for Folkestone. With its smart hotels and its Leas it is more of a seaside resort than a port. From the earliest times Folkestone's history has been that of a place by the sea. Before the war they dug up the remains of a Roman villa in the Warren — a rough tract on the cliffs — and found tiles stamped CL BR, which stands for *Classis Britannica*, the Latin for 'British Fleet', the history of which is an object lesson in the value of sea power. This so-called *Classis Britannica* was actually based on Boulogne, which the Romans called Gessoriacum. When the Roman Empire was in pretty fair chaos in the third century, the task of this fleet was to suppress piracy, particularly that of the Franks, and the admiral in command, Carausius, found a very satisfactory way (from his point of view) of doing this. When the pirate ships were outward bound down the Channel he anticipated Nelson and (in the spirit if not in the letter) put his blind eye to the telescope and let them pass; but when they reappeared homeward bound and laden down with booty, Carausius pounced on them and appropriated most of the booty for himself. When the Roman emperor heard about this he ordered Carausius to be removed from command and executed (no nonsense about civil rights in those days). This caused Carausius to rebel; by now a very rich man, he was able to pay the fleet well and keep it on his side. So great was the influence of sea power that he not only defied the emperor with impunity but took over the province of Britain as well, and ruled it as an independent sovereign. His fleets commanded the coasts of Europe right round to the Mediterranean, and it was eleven years before Constantius (the father of Constantine the Great), who had been made associate emperor, was able to recover Britain from Carausius's successor Allectus. Even then there was a certain amount of luck about it as Allectus's fleet became lost in a fog off the Isle of Wight, so that his opponents were able to slip by and land their army in the west country. The career of Carausius shows that even in the third century Britannia, given the chance, could rule the waves.

The churches both of Folkestone and of Hythe four miles away are noteworthy for having enormous collections of skulls and other human bones. In 456, we are told, a bloody battle was fought, at a spot between Folkestone and Hythe, by the Britons under King Vortimer and the Saxons who were retreating before him after their defeat on the banks of the Darent. On what evidence I know not, it is suggested that the bones at Hythe are those of the Britons and those at Folkestone those of the Saxons.

Folkestone has also a long history of fighting with Danish raiders – another reminder of what you suffer if you lose the mastery of the sea. Much of the town is owned by the Earl of Radnor, whose family name of Bouverie is given to the square where the bus station functions.

We all know what we owe to the pioneers of the medical profession, and Folkestone is famous as the birthplace of William Harvey, who discovered the circulation of the blood. He has his statue on the Leas and has left behind a curious story about his death. It is related that one morning he woke to find that he had gone stone blind. He had prepared himself against such a thing happening, and without turning a hair, after checking that his sight had in fact gone, he calmly sent for a bottle of poison, drank it and expired within three hours!

No vessels now ply between Folkestone and Hythe, another port that has 'had it'. Like Sandwich, it is a Cinque Port (pronounced 'sink'), but are they not (except Dover) 'sunk' ports? The waters receded and Hythe's former importance was at an end. You can't argue with the sea, as Canute demonstrated.

Hythe is simply a quiet resort and residential place. Its most interesting part is on the hillside from the church (which was a chapel of Saltwood) downwards; the main street runs at the foot. The collection of bones at the church cannot as a rule be seen by the public. The building is so well looked after that it smells of furniture polish. It has a chancel, like Canterbury Cathedral on a smaller scale, approached by ranges of steps from the nave. Saltwood people cannot claim that their church is any older than some parts of its former chapel of Hythe.

Anyone who has even a rough idea what Norman work is like will see that there is plenty of it in the latter church.

From Hythe you look out across the rich verdure of Romney Marsh, and the bay that rims it to the shingle point of Dungeness, and to the dark humps of the power stations. The marsh was deemed a defensive weakness by William Pitt who had the Royal Military Canal built, running on the landward side to protect England against Napoleon's Grand Army. But thanks to the Royal Navy this pipsqueak canal was never put to the test. On the coastal border of the marsh we still see the martello towers, built when the canal was made, for the same purpose.

Saltwood can claim to rank high in interest among Kentish villages. As well as an ancient church it has perhaps the finest medieval castle in the county, which is linked by tradition with the events leading to the martyrdom of Thomas Becket – only Canterbury Cathedral itself has a closer connection with them – and by complete contrast it has a great garden as beautiful as can be found anywhere in the world. And to add spice to the dish, it has the memory of James Croft. Taking these one by one, the castle goes back to before the Conquest. King Canute gave it to the monks of Christchurch at Canterbury, but it had been founded centuries before by

Saltwood Castle

Oisc, one of the early kings of Kent. It is partly restored so that it can be used to live in, but most of it is a ruin though fairly complete. Parts of the castle are called after Archbishop Courtenay who added a hall and a chapel in the reign of Richard II, but the walls and towers are much older than that. There are no archbishops there

67

now; old Cranmer, as part of his appeasement policy, handed it over to Henry VIII long, long ago. It is one of the best castles in private hands, and yet the public are allowed to visit it without having to get permission from some snooty estate agent. There are creepers growing on the walls and rambling roses sprouting from the crevices, which give the ruins such a picturesque charm compared with the gaunt, clean-scraped monuments that the Government looks after. It will be said that the creepers and the rose bushes are to some extent eating away the stonework; perhaps they are, but very, very slowly. And at Saltwood, for good measure, there are peacocks parading on the lawns, perching in the battlements, and surprising the visitors with their strange cries. There is scandal and mystery too. At the castle the rascally Ralph de Broc is supposed to have plotted with the four knights the murder of Thomas Becket in 1170. Some people – scientific historians – are now raising doubts about the story, but it seems to be supported by contemporary accounts.

The records of Saltwood church do not go back quite as far as those of the castle, but parts of it are Norman, and there are exciting funerary brasses: a priest, a knight, an angel and a medieval lady have their images perpetuated on the metal. A stained glass window is dedicated to Charlotte Croft, and this brings us to the skeleton in Saltwood's cupboard. James Croft (Charlotte's husband) was rector here for forty-seven years and at the same time held the following livings: Cliffe-at-Hoo (that is near Rochester), two livings at Sandwich and three at Canterbury, as well as Lympne, Teynham (near Sittingbourne), West Hythe, Stodmarsh, Lynsted, Doddington, Iwade and Chapel-of-Stone. His total income from his preferments approached £5,000 a year, and this early in the nineteenth century: it must have been equivalent to at least ten times that amount in our present money. All this ecclesiastical plunder was the reward of a most meritorious action – marrying the Archbishop of Canterbury's daughter – and the ample income did not in any way soften Croft's avarice. A letter has been preserved which shows him as being out for every penny he could screw out of the tithe-payers and ready to threaten legal action on the least sign of reluctance to pay up.

So much for the guilty secret of Saltwood; now for its most colourful glory, the flowering shrubs and trees.

About the middle of the last century a rich landowner employed an American gardener to plant his garden with trees and shrubs adapted to the boggy soil. The rarest and most beautiful specimens were imported, not only from California but also from the Himalayas, China and Japan – no expense was spared. They are still flourishing today;

there are rhododendrons of the most exotic hues – the ordinary plant is practically unseen – from deep scarlet to the purest white, often with the fairest and most delicate markings; with banks of flame-coloured, yellow and rose-pink azaleas adding to the pattern of colour the effect is dazzling, incredible, breath-taking to the visitors to whom the display is thrown open in spring and early summer. The sheer size of the trees – they cannot accurately be called shrubs – is enough to make you rub your eyes; some of them over-top full-grown forest trees such as oak and ash. Those who have knocked about the world a good deal say they have never seen anything quite like this. It has taken generations for this fantastic display to reach its glowing maturity; obviously the present owes a deep debt of gratitude to the man who made the beginnings of such a store of beauty for future generations to enjoy. Fortunately we are able to give his name – James Croft, Archdeacon and Rector. If there is a moral in this story, I am not quite sure what it is.

Folkestone, the Leas

69

CHAPTER FIVE

Viri Palustres, *or Marshmen All*

Romney Marsh proper is roughly triangular, ten miles or so long and perhaps five miles across the base, which is called Rhee Wall. If you include Walland Marsh and Denge Marsh (which is often assumed) and Guldeford Level over the border in Sussex the area is nearly doubled, but even so the distance from end to end is only about sixteen miles. At first sight it seems small compared with, say, the Downs or the Weald, and some people might think it was scarcely worth a complete chapter. How wrong they would be! More than one writer has found material in it to fill a whole volume, there are so many topics to explore – the ups and downs of the earth's surface over millions of years that have created the marsh; the vicissitudes of the River Rother and its changing courses; the geological dimension – the muddy deposits and buried forests – the mysteries of the shingle accumulation of Dungeness, and the strange flora that it nourishes; the special farming qualities of the marsh land, and the fame of the Romney sheep; the innumerable migratory bird visitors, and the efforts to stimulate their number and variety; and strange human activities such as, a generation ago, the laying of the overseas pipeline, PLUTO, and today the nuclear power stations, a toy railway, rifle ranges and an airport; even the practice of sand-yachting. All these fill out the pages of marshland writers, not to mention the naturalists' wonderland of Camber sands and the antique charms of Rye town, both of which lie across the border in Sussex. And as the town of New Romney is custodian of some of the most important records of the Cinque Ports, the affairs of that ancient confederation can legitimately be included. So too the 'Lords of the Marsh' cannot be overlooked. Their manors, in rights of which their authority rested, included such places as Aldington, Bilsington, Bonnington, Ruckinge, Warehorne and other villages circling but not actually within the limits of the marsh. The truth is that a single chapter is not sufficient to explore in any detail all these manifold aspects of Romney Marsh, and for most of them a passing reference will have to do.

The newer Walland and Denge Marshes have been reclaimed only since the twelfth century when Archbishop Thomas Becket, zealous as ever for the interests of the Church, made the first 'inning' or

Dungeness lighthouse

that Palstre Court on the Isle of Oxney derives its name from this Latin expression.

The different courses of the Rother from Roman times onward can only be adequately illustrated with the aid of maps and diagrams; but (to put the matter as simply as possible by using the modern placenames) one can say that in Roman times the river flowed past Appledore and then divided into two channels, one reaching the sea at Hythe and the other at Romney; then the northern, or Hythe channel silted up, leaving the Appledore–Romney course only. Later, in the reign of Edward I, there was a terrible tempest that not only washed away Winchelsea as it then was but also altered completely the course of the Rother, so that instead of going round the north of the Isle of Oxney (which is even less of an island today than the Isle of Thanet) to Reading Street and Appledore, it took a right turn to the south and thence made its way to the present mouth near the modern Rye Harbour. Winchelsea was, incidentally, rebuilt on higher ground.

The best soil of the marsh produces a lush vegetation which in spring and early summer clothes it in a bright, almost violent, green, which tones down by autumn to a rich olive. The roads, before the days of competent highway engineering, were very wide, being merely pieces of the marsh fenced off, and were unpleasant to

enclosure of land for the monks of Christchurch, but Romney Marsh proper has existed throughout historical times. In a grant of King Offa of Mercia to Archbishop Janibert in the year 795, or thereabouts, the place is called Merscware, which was the name of the inhabitants, i.e. marsh men, or in Latin *Viri Palustres*. One writer claims

71

travel along after rain; now they are well surfaced, but extremely narrow and winding, as most of them thread along the banks of some watercourse.

The marsh has its own breed of sheep, and you will see vast flocks of them all over it. The Romney is a big sheep, but has to be crossed with other breeds to produce the best meat and wool. Hundreds of the Romney rams are exported yearly to all parts of the world for breeding. There is a mystique surrounding the pasturage of these animals; in spring when the grass is plentiful it is a point of honour that the rate of growth should not outpace the nibbling by the sheep. The prudent farmer throws a coin as far as he can across the pasturage, and if he cannot then see it, the grass is too long. Sheep it is said, like grass which grew yesterday, not last week. This is how the moderates put it; the more extreme pundits say that the sheep like to see their breakfast growing.

The tendency is for the acreages under the plough to increase, and for that under permanent grass to contract. Correspondingly, the number of sheep is decreasing, but there were so many thousands at the peak that the casual visitor would never suspect this.

The rich soil of the marsh is very suitable for market gardening. Many Lincolnshire horticulturalists found this out when the microscopic eel-worm ruined their land in that county. They had to look for pastures new, and found precisely these at Romney. There they gave a new boost to market gardening, and introduced the cultivation of bulbs, especially daffodils and tulips.

In olden times the marsh was thinly inhabited, being described by Lambarde as "bad in winter, worse in summer, and at no time good, only fit for those vast herds of cattle which feed all over it." The prevalence of "ague", or as we should call it malaria, meant that no one lived on the marsh unless they were forced to by their "mean condition". The wealthy land-owners lived in neighbouring towns or upland country, and the marsh villages consisted of handfuls of houses clustering round the churches. Today one cannot see any difference between the marshmen and other Kent people; not many wealthy stockbrokers may live there, but the marsh is no longer shunned.

Even the older parts of the marsh were dependent on sea-walling, embankments and unobstructed waterways for their safety, and this fact led to disputes about who should pay for these necessary works. In the end, King Henry III sent a judge, Henry de Bathe, who was clearly possessed of considerable administrative as well as legal skill, to draw up with local assistance a series of ordinances for the regulation of the marsh. These were so salutary that they endured for centuries until modern legislation took their place. In the meantime they had been copied in all other low-lying and marshy areas throughout the realm, not excluding Walland and Denge Marshes. Edward IV dotted the i's and crossed the t's of these regulations and set up a corporation consisting of the inhabitants, which gave them one seat on the organization called the 'Lords of the Marsh', the other twenty-three seats being held by the owners of the manors in and adjoining it. And, to encourage 'a better sort' to settle in the marsh, the inhabitants were granted "the privileges of leet, lawday and tourn, the exemption from toll and theam, and from so many other charges that hardly any other place in England had the like." The Lords of the Marsh and the Corporation held their meetings at the New Hall in Dymchurch, rebuilt in Elizabethan times, still there to see just near the church, and still used by those who manage the land drainage of the district. But they operate under some new-fangled set-up much different from, and, one can safely wager, a good deal more expensive than, the wholesome ordinances of Henry de Bathe.

In the days of turnpikes and stage-coaches the high road from Romney to Hythe ran along the top of Dymchurch Wall, so wide and strong and reliable was this man-made embankment that kept the sea out of Romney Marsh. The Dymchurch Wall is still there today but the road now runs below it, while the Wall, strengthened (we hope) by modern engineering, carries a pathway that gives an exhilarating, breezy promenade with fine views across the bay formed by the curving sweep of coast from Dungeness to the Folkestone heights. The ebbing tide leaves a broad expanse of firm, clean sand to please the many holidaymakers of summer, and the solitary walkers of other seasons. The crest of the Wall quite overtops the houses on its landward side. Only here and there, as in the centre of Dymchurch, has any building other than a martello tower, a redoubt or a look-out point a view of the sea. The ocean and the sand attract, but the masking of the view by the sea wall discourages the holidaymaker; it is therefore the less exacting type of client who comes here to patronize the numerous holiday camps, a whole string of which mark this coast. The houses that people build tend also to be of the more modest sort, not excluding the ubiquitous bungalow. Some kind of rag-tag defence installation and a gravel plant tend to lower still further the general tone of this coast, which however recovers momentarily in the older part of Dymchurch, where the church and Old Hall have a few houses of character to keep them company. Eventually the nightmare (for it *is* something of a nightmare for the more aesthetic, to drive along this road) ends when the golfers take over the coastline beyond St Mary's Bay. Here the road swings inland to

73

New Romney church

St Nicholas, its outside richly arcaded in the style of the twelfth century and its interior a museum-piece of box pews, ledger stones and brasses, now presides without rival over a quiet country town. It was not always so; when the Cinque Ports were in their heyday there were five parish churches as well as a priory, and a hospital for the sick.

There is dignified eighteenth-century architecture in the High Street, culminating in Priory House; also in the Church Approach, where the Assembly Rooms rub shoulders with the even earlier school of 1676. And New Romney has much else to interest us — two sets of eighteenth-century almshouses for instance, until it is time to go on to Lydd.

Here is another great church, and an even quieter dignity of townscape. This is an isolated community, besieged between the marshlands and the moon-landscape of Dungeness, the airport and the military firing-ranges, the last outpost of urbanity before science, applied or misapplied, takes over. As you walk round, one 'square', often triangular, leads to another. High Street, Turney Hall, Coronation Square, Skinner Street, the Ripe — these are the names you find in Lydd. It is a trite saying that All Saints' church is the cathedral of the marsh; it entrances both the architect and the

the little town of New Romney, standing about a mile from the sea, with the old Romney Warren, now Littlestone Golf Course, protecting its northern flank from invasion.

So New Romney has not been submerged by the tide of caravans and chalets. The splendid Norman church of archaeologist. Its great length and lofty vaulting do not by themselves account for the nickname. The very style of building is reminiscent of a cathedral; the fifteenth-century tower, for example, has lierne vaulting such as is seen in Canterbury's nave, and the tower arch overlooking the nave is of stately proportions. The reason for the nickname is simple: the tower was actually built under the direction of one of the master-masons from Canterbury Cathedral. In the north-west corner, built into the walls, are traces of a Saxon predecessor.

We may be tempted to forget that in the last war Lydd was in the front line and suffered severely. A high explosive bomb, luckily one of modest size, scored a direct hit on the chancel of All Saints, completely destroying that part of the church, so that what we now see is a skilful rebuild. But while all was in ruin, human nature asserted itself and a soldier from one of the nearby camps helped himself to the funerary brass of Clement Stuppeny which had come adrift from its tomb. This trophy he bore off, but when about to embark for Normandy he gave it to a comrade. The new possessor took it home and eventually his wife, having heard perhaps some vague account of the history of the relic, wrote to the mayor of Lydd to see if he could throw any light on the subject. To make the irony all the greater, the then mayor was one of the churchwardens of Lydd

Lydd

church! What next happened we can perhaps imagine, but all's well that ends well, and the brass, only a little the worse for its adventures, is now attached once more to Stuppeny's tomb. He died, by the way, in 1608.

The vast shingle area of Denge Beach is varied only by some open 'pits' full of water – which I am assured is not salt or even brackish, but fresh, though I would not risk

75

putting it in *my* whisky — and occasional sparse vegetation, the 'holme trees' recorded by our ancient writers and called by the moderns 'holly tops', broom, thrift and even foxgloves. When the sun shines the explorer can seek out these plants and shrubs, and enjoy the little splashes of colour they bring; but when the south-west gales lash the headland, bringing sheets of driving rain and confining the visitor to the roads, he sees a landscape whose colours remind him only of jungle camouflage — a dirty brown with formless green and black mottling.

On the point of Dungeness itself the ten-fathom channel comes close inshore and the shipping seems almost to scrape the shingle. The comings and goings of the lifeboatmen, coastguards and the occasional fishermen are made tolerable only by duck-boards over the pebbles. In the background loom three huge dark shapes, the buildings of the power stations.

This is the grimmest, barrenest picture to be found in and around Romney Marsh; yet we are only a mile or two from Lydd, where all is peaceful, fruitful and green.

The route that we have followed so far has shown the seamy side of Romney Marsh, relieved by the oases of New Romney and Lydd. It requires only a small difference of itinerary to see the best instead of the worst; the start is on the heights above West Hythe. On the crest of the steep hill that runs down from the Lympne road stands a tall stone cross, rather like a war memorial, the Shepway Cross. Whether or not this monument stands, as alleged, on the exact spot where the chief court of the Cinque Ports used to meet, there is no doubt that it is on a superb site; there could be no finer one than this lofty position with a great view of the English Channel, of Romney Marsh and of Dungeness, and there could be no better starting point for an exploration of the quieter reaches of the marsh.

Along the foot of the escarpment here runs the Military Canal and the village of West Hythe straggles beside it, once a great harbour at the mouth of the River Limen (or Rother) but now insignificant, even its church a ruin. Half a mile further south, at Botolph's Bridge, five winding roads converge, two of which lead onward into the heart of the marsh. One of these keeps within a mile of the canal and the escarpment, with Lympne Castle and church on the skyline, and Stutfall Castle, as the remains of the Roman fort of Lemanis are called, scattered about the hillside below.

Let us take, for the moment, the other marshland road which brings you in something over a mile to Burmarsh, where the church, typical of its kind, is a good introduction to the marsh. Its walls and entrance doorway are Norman, and inside it is simple, small and

mpne, church and castle

To reach your next village you will have to come back almost to the coast at Dymchurch before setting off again into the blue, or rather the green, following the signposts for St Mary-in-the-Marsh, and hoping to find a village as delightful as its own name. The church, in fact, tries in its quiet, unassuming way to fulfil these hopes. The Norman tower, with its tiny Norman windows, has great buttresses tiled like a roof, and the Victorian restorers have let it off lightly. But it stands at the corner of a road leading to nowhere in particular, and has for company only a group of standardized council houses and a little pub.

Beyond St Mary's the road leads on with no more than a couple of sharp corners to Old Romney, passing on the roadside Honeychild Manor, an unromantic-looking farm, and at a distance of a mile, the pathetic ruins of All Saints, a reminder of the defunct parish of Hope.

There is something haunting and appealing about a church set amid grass fields, with only a house or two anywhere near at hand. There is rarely another person in sight when one visits Old Romney, though you may have to shoo away some groups of grazing sheep to reach the churchyard gate. The church is a building of the past rather than the present; the prosperous port it served has simply disappeared and there remain only a collection of weathered gravestones and a centuries-old yew, looking

intimate, befitting the peace of the marsh. Disconcertingly, one of the windows has been restored in memory of a former rector found drowned in a dyke. Of more pleasant interest, there is a showcase which has a Breeches Bible, a pewter flagon, and photographs of the inside of the church as it was nearly a century ago, before 'restoration'.

as big as the church itself. The interior, as at St Mary's, has escaped the attention of the Victorian renovators and so keeps its old flavour, with box pews, minstrels' gallery and ancient font. A fine ledger stone commemorates a Frenchman, a Huguenot refugee who was rector for forty-eight years from 1690.

From Old Romney a byroad leads – about as curly as a corkscrew – past more abandoned ruins, this time of Midley church, to Lydd.

In the mind's eye we must now go back to Botolph's Bridge and take the second marshland road which started out roughly parallel to the military canal. Picking its way among the deep ditches, the route begins to edge away from the canal as it makes towards Sherlock's Bridges, where there is another parting of the ways. A byroad leads into Dymchurch passing two ruins, those of Eastbridge and Orgarswick churches, whose parishes no longer exist separately, though services are held each year, at Rogationtide, amid the crumbling walls. By going forward and making a jink to left and to right the traveller can find the road to Newchurch, a mile further on; the large church, built of Kentish rag, leaves no sharp impression in the memory. It has been described as 'over-restored'. Nearly 200 years ago, Hasted had the same feeling: "Nothing further worth mentioning", he declared, after writing of a few straggling houses.

The Newchurch road, with sundry turns and small diversions, will take you on to Ivychurch, which has one of the largest village churches in the country, vying with All Saints in Lydd town for pre-eminence within the marsh. The history of its buildings and rebuildings is specially interesting. In its present form it was constructed during the reign of Edward III, just when St George was recognized as the patron saint of England; hence, probably, the dedication of the church to him. Many famous or notorious men figure in the list of its rectors; the church's booklet sets it all out and makes good reading. At the turn of the century the building was terribly neglected, evil-smelling, open to the sky in many places, walls tottering and windows stuffed with sacking, a haven much appreciated by hordes of mice, bats and owls. It is still under restoration and the impression is that of a vast, bare, ecclesiastical barn with furnishings and signs of activity tucked away at the east end.

Ivychurch is on the main New Romney–Ashford road; pressing on across country you will come on to the New Romney–Tenterden road near Brenzett.

So poor are the main roads in Romney Marsh that four miles of this highway heading *north*-west are a link in the main cross-marsh road running *south*-west from Hythe to Rye. At Brenzett, the Tenterden traffic goes straight on,

Brookland church

but that for Rye (the main stream which we follow) turns off at one of those many dangerously sharp angles that make the A259 a disgrace to the 'Department of the Environment'. Within less than a mile one reaches the next pair of right-angled turns and, more pleasantly, Brookland, the star village of Walland Marsh. Hasted says of Brookland that the village is neat and rather pleasant considering the situation (not a bad description of it today). "The houses", he adds, "as well as inhabitants, are of a better sort than are usually seen in the Marsh." The church gains three stars, one for its belfry, detached and entirely wooden (the main timbers are two feet square), roofed with shingles, with three conical storeys described as being like three candle snuffers stacked one on another — would not a more familiar comparison now be traffic cones?

Tradition has it that the belfry was once on the church but fell off in surprise when a virgin came to be married. If we are to believe this, and also what Hasted says about the superiority of the inhabitants of Brookland, it does not say much for the morals of the rest of the marsh! It is supposed that the Victorians forgot to restore Brookland so that, both outside and in, the church is a feast of eccentricities. The second of our stars we award to the lead font, from every point of view superb — unique in fact in Britain; nearly 800 years old, it

is decorated with delightful vignettes of the signs of the zodiac and the labours of the months. Any one of half-a-dozen objects could claim the third star. I would put first the wall painting — which has survived by accident behind a later memorial now removed — of the murder of Becket, which is said to be fifteenth century. The architecture of the church is ancient and pleasing and there are box pews and medieval benches. Shown with great pride is the movable graveside shelter, a kind of wooden sentry-box to keep the minister dry at funerals, and the weights and scales of the Hundred of Alloes Bridge, dated 1795; also the ancient tithe pen, a brass, and several ledger stones.

Tucked away in the north-western corner of the marsh are Fairfield and Snargate, and if on the way north you take the Ashford road you will pass through the village street of Snave. Perhaps I may leave the reader to explore these places for himself; they are just typical marshland villages.

Earlier, something was said about the Lords of Romney Marsh. They were the squires of certain villages. Not all of these were in the marsh itself; some were keeping an eye on it from the rising ground around its margin, either — like Lympne and Aldington — from a commanding height on the Quarry Hills, or from more gentle elevations such as Bilsington and Bonnington.

Lympne is one of those villages just off the beaten track. You can go past it year after year and think that its outer fringes, which are all that you see, are the village itself, scarcely noticing the narrow opening between a couple of cottages that leads to the church, the castle and the true heart of the village. The narrow road twists behind high walls as if determined to keep to itself the secret of the way to Lympne, and comes at last to a dead end. The gateway of the churchyard is in front of you, the gateway of the castle on your right – choose one building or the other, or go home, the choice is yours.

The church is a typical thirteenth-century building, much restored, solid looking, and a great landmark when seen from the northern parts of Romney Marsh which it overlooks, and over which there is a magnificent and famous view from the churchyard. The castle is such only by courtesy, and its battlements are only decorative; it is really a former manor house and residence of the archdeacons of Canterbury, dating from the fifteenth century. It and the church make a spectacular group. A mile or so away is the ruined chapel of Court-at-Street, with memories of Elizabeth Barton, the Holy Maid of Kent. Her sanctity was not however appreciated by Henry VIII who sent her to her doom at Tyburn.

No one who has been to Aldington needs to scratch his head in order to remember the village and its church.

The latter is on high ground, prominent from all sides; it is a large one; the tower begun in 1507 was only finished in 1911; and Erasmus was rector here for a short time. The Court Lodge, next door, was once the manor house of the archbishop. It has a neat stone-built Victorian front and an interesting but untidy rear, with Gothic tracery built into the brick-and-stone wall where the chapel once stood. A good-natured sheepdog, blind in one eye, and a number of somnolent geese, with a background of rolling countryside, complete the peaceful scene.

Continuing to skirt the marsh anti-clockwise, the road brings you to Bonnington. Unless you are interested in penal reform and detention there is nothing much to interest you except the church again, which along with those of Bilsington, Ruckinge and Warehorne can be remembered because it has a slight disadvantage or handicap. Bonnington church is away from the village amid fields, down the hill beside the Royal Military Canal, and is encumbered with a strange and unusual dedication – to the Saxon saint Rumwold. The saint's reputation for piety would perhaps be more convincing had he not died at the age of three – days, not years.

Bilsington church is also down the hill; from St Rumwold's, to avoid having to turn you can take a short tour of the marsh and approach Bilsington from the south, whence church and court lodge can be seen hiding coyly in a dense thicket. There is a most satisfactory moat round the old court lodge farm; it has deep water and is the haunt of many ducks. The church is old — what village church in Kent is not — and its handicap is a weak tower which could not support the weight of its two bells. So one of them was brought down and hung outside near the west end of the church on a frame, protected by a sort of dovecote. On the other side of the road from the church and court lodge is the monument (now partly wrecked by lightning) to Sir William Casway, killed by falling off a stagecoach.

Ruckinge and Warehorne are the last two extra-mural lordships of the marsh that we have to look at. The former church's misfortune is to have been seriously damaged by fire, years and years ago. Why it was not properly repaired we do not know, but we hope that it was not another case like Goudhurst and Wingham (as you will hear) of the money disappearing. Anyhow, the inside stonework is badly flaked, and the walls are bare of all memorials and tablets; the beams also look more than rough-hewn, perhaps charred in the conflagration. Yet the general effect is one of rugged, primitive charm, not altogether displeasing.

Warehorne is another of those tiny villages on a by-lane off the main road, so little spoilt that it is necessary to place a small 'Lyons Maid' ice-cream sign on the verge as a hint of where to start looking for the village shop, not otherwise visible. The body of the church is a classic example of Decorated architecture, with what I believe is called 'intersecting' window tracery. The cross it has to bear (if the metaphor is not improper in this context) is that of having a tower and porch incongruously constructed in staring red brick: they date from the eighteenth century but look more modern. Just opposite the place where the village road turns off the high road is a large, impressive, well-preserved building as clean and neat as a doll's house; this is Leacon Hall, dating from the reign of Queen Anne.

Appledore church, on the edge of the marsh, has a certain gloomy grandeur. It is very large, with much screening and panelling, but lighter, brighter and the most interesting is the Horne chapel, once the property of a family who lost out through backing the wrong horse at the Reformation. Their old home, Horne's Place, lies off the road from Appledore to Warehorne; out of sight at the rear is its most ancient part, the private chapel.

Kent lures you on; inspecting the lordships of the marsh we were enticed to Appledore, which is not one of them (enticed, incidentally, from the road to Woodchurch, which we must investigate another time).

Appledore

unusual concave-sided pillars in its nave; opposite is the Lutyens-designed Wittersham House, described as 'suavely neo-Georgian', and in the next breath as possessing a 'syncopated' fenestration. To us ordinary folk Wittersham House seems to have an attractive 'something'.

At Stone-in-Oxney to the east overlooking the Military Canal, the church, whose surroundings are particularly delightful at daffodil-time, serves also as the local museum; under the tower are assembled a Roman Mithraic altar, very battered, and with a ring-bolt giving a hint of its misadventures; also the fossilized bones of an iguanodon's tail, and the similarly petrified scales of a prehistoric pike!

Two special topics we have reserved for the end of the chapter, the Cinque Ports and the nuclear power stations. So much has been written on the Ports that a glossary of the technical terms and legal expressions seems to be all that is required to refresh the reader's mind, and perhaps to enable him to talk with a convincing air of knowledge about them. Here it is:

Coronation Privileges. The right to carry a canopy over the king, and to dine at his table. Both discontinued because the king (or queen) now goes to the Abbey in a coach, and the Coronation Banquet no longer takes

Now that we are in Appledore we see a sign 'Stone' – Stone-in-Oxney! Having come so far we cannot resist the beckoning of the isle. We already know of Palstre Court – now a white-rendered farmhouse – and its alleged connection with the *Viri Palustres*; the chief village on the island is Wittersham. Down the lane that leads into Sussex is a church with a handsome tower and

83

place. But when Coronation Barons of the different Cinque Ports get together they can sometimes be heard to speak of the time when some of their number (naturally not those from the speaker's town) let the side down by getting drunk and making rather a hash of carrying the canopy, so that this little episode was cut out of subsequent coronations.

Den and Strond. The right to land catch and dry nets at Great Yarmouth.

Coronation Barons. Men (virtually never lords) deputed to attend the Coronation on behalf of the Cinque Ports.

Court of Shepway. Superior court of the Confederation, called after the Lathe of Shepway.

Lord Warden. Officer who presided at the Court of Shepway and is invariably also appointed Constable of Dover Castle, but in later years has been merely the holder of an honorary distinction, with the right to live at Walmer Castle.

Brotherhood and Guestling. Name of the meeting of all the Corporate members of the Cinque Ports (i.e. including 'limbs' such as Lydd, Faversham, etc.). Nothing to do with brotherhood or guests, but derived from the names of the villages where the courts were first held.

Black and White Books. In which the transactions of the Court of Brotherhood and Guestling were recorded.

A technical description of the nuclear processes would be outside the design of this book, but we took advantage of an offer to show us round Dungeness A. Protons, neutrons and electrons play an indispensable part, it seems, in the nuclear operation, spurred into action by uranium and graphite, in a critical condition, apparently, but somewhat restrained by a judicious addition of boron. The emanations of these hideously dangerous processes are intercepted, and prevented from injuring human beings, by a 'biological shield' of thick concrete. Behind this shield is a state of affairs rather like 'the house that Jack built'; the reactor heats up gases which in their turn heat the water which is turned into steam, which drives the huge turbo-alternators that generate the electricity! The voltage is fantastically high, and it has to be transformed down to a more reasonable figure at which it can be fed into the national grid. The station now operating has two reactors; Dungeness B has been under construction for years now, but one is not told of a date for completion.

In the flat landscape of the marsh, the lines of pylons leading from Dungeness, north to Canterbury and west towards Sussex, have perhaps a certain repetitious rhythm, but however hard one tries, remembering always the benefits that electricity brings, it is difficult to see any beauty in them.

CHAPTER SIX

The Downs so Free

"Yes; it *was* pleasant enough here," said a farmer friend of mine, as he paused on his doorstep. "A case, as you might say, of 'every prospect pleases', but you know what the next line is. Now we have *that* to look at!" He nodded toward the distant downland where a great white chalky gash had been drawn across the green hillside; work had started on the new bypass of the village. "You wouldn't get a farmer doing a thing like that. He will never do anything to desecrate the countryside; it would go against his deepest instincts. Farming is woven into the life of the community, not a thing separate and apart like a commercial business. The farmer and his farm are part and parcel of the land, like the other people who live on it."

It was stimulating and encouraging to hear this, although it is a moot point as to what does or does not desecrate the countryside. You can get used to a lot of things that come into your daily round, but which may startle a newcomer. As he was speaking the farmer was scraping his gumboots with a stick to remove some of the mud he had accumulated in walking through the ankle-deep mire from the barns to his front door. He was in a big way of business and the substantial buildings from the storage of fruit and boxes were ranged behind the house. Some were of the corrugated iron age; the more modern ones had roofs of asbestos, only slightly mellowed by a mottling of lichen; all looked to be in need of a lick of paint except for one brand-new brightly tinted specimen made of what looked like sheet steel. On the way to the farm I had noticed silos of gleaming aluminium in the fields. All were in some degree unsightly but all were necessary for carrying on the life of Britain. So, possibly, was the bypass!

The North Downs are rather a large area to describe. Kent's backbone, they have been called, extending all the way from Halstead right on the Greater London boundary to the celebrated White Cliffs over fifty miles away. I am speaking of the Kent section of them, naturally. I am not quite clear how far the name extends in the other direction, but if North Downs Way is any guide it must carry through as far as Farnham. At the London end they are quite narrow, not more than a couple of miles across, but as they get nearer the Channel the Downs widen out; and if you take a line from Walmer to Folkestone, which represents their greatest width, it is about twelve miles as the crow flies. If you look at the Downs from the south or south-west they are quite unmistakable with their steep escarpment rising in places to a height of 800 feet, but from the northern side they rise only gradually and there is no steep hill to show where they begin. The ascent above Boughton Street as you travel east is caused by a projecting spur of the downland, whose features include the remains of the forest of Blean and the chalk cliffs of Thanet.

As we are merely selecting an area for purposes of our description we can be a little arbitrary, and, whether geographically correct or not, take the line of Watling Street from Dartford through Rochester to Canterbury as the northern boundary of the Downs. At Canterbury the road changes direction and heads actually across the Downs to Dover; here we must be even more arbitrary and take an imaginary line from Canterbury to Deal as the demarcation.

Now farming-wise the best land in Kent is just north of Watling Street between Rainham and Faversham. Here you will get orchards, especially cherries and pears, hop-gardens, soft fruit (strawberries and raspberries) and vegetables. Its excellence has been recognized since the time of Henry VIII when Richard Harris, the king's

fruiterer, planted apples and cherries to make us independent of foreign supplies. He was the pioneer of the modern orchard with the trees standing "in most right line" and "of one sorte, shape, and fashion, as if they had beene drawen thorow one Mould ... " So says Lambarde, and on the opposite page under the heading "Tenham" is another of his oft-quoted passages:

> For heere have wee, not onely the most dainty piece of all our Shyre, but such a Singularitie as the whole British Iland is not able to patterne. The Ile of Thanet, and those Easterne parts, are the Grayner: the Weald was the Wood: Rumney Marsh, is the Medow plot: the Northdownes towards the Thamyse, be the Cony garthe, or Warreine: and this Tenham with thirty other parishes (lying on each side this porte way, and extending from Raynham to Blean Wood) bee the Cherrie gardein, and Apple orcharde of Kent.

South of the "porte way", now dubbed the A2, the land gradually rises and the Downs, as we have defined them, begin. You still have your orchards and hop-gardens but the land is not of the same superb quality. You get an intermittent turning over to chalk, clay and flint: so there is more arable and even pasture; but the Downs are seamed with little valleys which have pockets of better land. If you ask how the Downs compare in fertility with, say, Romney Marsh I can only say that you cannot make a fair comparison; it is like saying which is

86

Chillenden Mill, near Eastry

the better, sherry or champagne.

The pattern of agriculture is always changing. You read in the old books of the grubbing-up of orchards and hop-gardens in places where today they flourish better than ever. Fashions in fruit alter with the eating habits of the public and also with the financial climate, and now

according to the views and decisions of the EEC bureaucrats. With the removal of the protection they used to have, hops are now less important and fruit is more at risk, while some crops – plums and cherries – are a bit of a gamble. There are diseases such as silver leaf in plums which are incurable and it is a matter of luck how long you can carry on with your trees before they become infected, at least to some extent. We in Kent have special problems because our crops are capital intensive. Even women's lib affects us; the dear ladies no longer give us a pool of cheap labour, and we have to do everything we can to cut down the need for it, such as growing smaller trees.

The subjects that we have picked for our illustrations show in a very practical way how the quality of the land influences human life. Most of our subjects we unconsciously selected from the places where the land is the most fertile, which means more money, more prosperity, bigger churches, better buildings.

Taking then the Downs from west to east, we can begin at the Darent. The section between it and the Medway is pleasant enough, but is chopped into three by two very busy roads, the London/Dover alternative to Watling Street, the A20, running through from Farningham to Wrotham, bringing a good deal of ribbon development, the Brands Hatch motor race track and the Wrotham television mast. Away from the main roads the country is as pretty and pleasant as any in Kent, but you cannot go more than a mile or two before you hit one of them or run out into the industrial area along the estuary. Stansted is a delightful little spot; the charming hill and dale country continues through to Hartley and Longfield, and at North Ash is a valiant experiment in fitting modern housing into a rural setting. New Ash Green, a sort of private enterprise new town, is I believe well esteemed in architectural circles of the more progressive kind.

The second road dividing this part of the Downs is the Gravesend–Wrotham one which runs through Nurstead and Meopham. Nurstead Court is a famous old building but the ancient section was partly demolished in the nineteenth century when the present house was built. At Meopham there are many of the elements good and bad that make up the countryside of this part of the Downs. The station, nearer to Nurstead than to Meopham, brings commuters; tarmacked and kerbed roads with modern houses introduce a suburban dimension. But the place is strung out, and at the south end is a real village green with a windmill, the least spoilt part. The impressive church hides in disapproval behind a clump of trees. But who can blame the commuters for wanting to have it both ways – a job in town by day, and a medieval church, village green and windmill to come home to in the evening, with all mod. cons thrown in? They can likewise reflect on the high honour of living in a place which as long ago as AD 940 Athelstan, King of England, permitted Duke Edulf to give to the monks of Canterbury; an example followed some years later by one Byrhtric, a rich and powerful man who gave the monks not only land but thirty marks, one necklace of twenty marks and two cups of silver.

The road goes on to Wrotham, and from the top of Wrotham Hill (on the London Road) is a magnificent view of the Medway valley and the North Downs in one direction and of the Quarry Hills and the Weald beyond in the other. Wrotham itself is halfway down the hill, bypassed by the London Road, but with the Tonbridge–Gravesend highway running through it. The embryonic square, flanked by the large church and the Elizabethan Wrotham Place, is a little maze of traffic islands and signs, and the Place has been spruced up and divided into office suites. The archbishops of Canterbury once had a palace or manor house here, and a large stone dwelling has been made out of the remains of it to the east of the church. These archiepiscopal residences were rather like the modern motels, for the use of Their Graces when making their progresses about the country, and it was while at Wrotham that Archbishop Richard in the twelfth century had a vision of the Almighty, who told him in no uncertain terms of the unfavourable view taken at headquarters of his shortcomings, which gave the poor man the horrors. He pushed on to Halling, the next post-house on the way back to Canterbury, where, overcome by his experience, he gave up the ghost.

Between the Gravesend–Wrotham road and the valley of the Medway is the pocket of hilly country round Luddesdown and Buckland, quite a remote, peaceful, wooded area whose narrow roads tend to keep it so, but it is in the northern skirts of these hills that we have the brightest jewel of the downland west of the Medway – the village of Cobham, with its threefold attractions of the church, the old college and the Hall. The church is very interesting architecturally, but for most of us, its vaulting and pillars are merely a background for the most wonderful collection of brasses in the country and a famous and magnificent tomb. The chancel of Cobham has what amounts to a wall-to-wall carpet of funerary brass, a solid mass of no less than fourteen arranged in two rows of the lords of Cobham and their wives, and in the case of the women, of their husbands, plus one priest. The Cobhams had no false modesty and in 1558 they put the tomb of George Brooke Lord Cobham and his wife slap in the middle of the chancel, and a fine tomb it is, especially for those of us who like to see a bit of heraldic colour

Cobham Hall

livening up the grey stonework of our churches.

Behind Cobham church are the remains of the New College. The name is a bit misleading as the buildings, although they date from 1370, have been used for the last four hundred years or so as almshouses. The stately mansion of Cobham Hall in its park to the east of the church is now used as a girls' school. Thank goodness that this impressive monument to the wealth and power

89

of the Lords of Cobham has been found useful to the modern generation. It would be a tragedy if it suffered the same fate as the more or less contemporary mansion of Shurland on the Isle of Sheppey, of which only a fragment remains. In the village, just near the church, is the local inn The Leather Bottle which claims to have associations with Dickens.

There are so many interesting things to describe that our progress across the Downs may be rather leisurely, and from Darent to Medway is a mere ten miles. We still have over twenty miles to the Stour, and beyond that another twenty or so of a much wider tableland to the coast.

East of the Medway, once you are outside the influence of the Medway towns, the Downs become much more solitary, deserted and remote, and in places they have an open look, not unlike the Yorkshire Wolds. The industrial influence is soon lost. Bredhurst, for instance, is half village, half suburb, beside the M2, but a mile or two further east, almost in sight of the motorway, there is the fascinating countryside round Guildsted, Hill Green and Queen Down Warren. The warren is indeed a place of some mystery with its little network of single track roads and in spring endless vistas of daffodils and narcissi, ten times the number that Wordsworth could ever have seen. At Hill Green there

is a farm for all the world like one in the heart of the Weald, with its black and white half-timbering; but the roadside verges are trimmed like a croquet lawn, peacocks wander around, and Jaguars and Mercedes are parked near the front door. Within minutes from here is the austere wind-blown hilltop of Stockbury, with big church, little bungalows and vanished castle. Hucking, Bicknor, Frinsted — these are all typical downland villages in what Hasted described as a cold and dreary country, but we like their solitude and their integrity that comes through surviving the centuries. We also like the names of the old manors — Yokes Court, Madam's Court and Morning Dawn.

As the land sinks northward below the hundred-foot contour and the little valleys widen out we get a more broken, varied and enclosed country with the motorway cutting through it, but affecting it little, or not at all — just an occasional glimpse as our car flashes under or over a bridge. We have reminders of very early Saxon origins in '-ing' places — Wichling and Eastling, for instance. Eastling used to be noted for an unusual sport called squirrel hunting, held on 30th November in each year when, says a contemporary account,

labourers and lower kind of people assembling together form a lawless rabble and being accoutred with guns, poles, clubs and other such weapons spend the greatest part of the day in parading through the woods and grounds with loud shoutings and under the pretence of demolishing the squirrels, some few of which they kill, they destroy numbers of hares, pheasants, partridges and in short whatever comes in their way, breaking down the hedges and doing much other mischief, and in the evening partaking themselves to the ale houses to finish their career there in drunkenness as is usual with such sort of gentry.

Lynsted, in the heart of the orchard country, has in its church sculptured monuments that are famous, particularly the tomb of Lord Teynham, done by the celebrated Jacobean sculptor Epiphanius Evesham, a down-to-earth English Michelangelo. He shows Lord Teynham with the serene expression of one who knows that his credentials are in order to pass the pearly gates, while his widow's face is lined with nobly restrained grief, and on a smaller scale around the side of his tomb the family cry their eyes out. The slight hill shows off to advantage the church and the timbered houses around it, whilst scattered about the neighbouring orchards are the gentlemen's seats of the sixteenth, seventeenth and eighteenth centuries, hiding themselves amid the orchards like windfall bramleys in the paddock grass. At Provender, Prince and Princess Romanoff proudly claim that their house, large, impressive and half-timbered, with huge fireplaces within centuries older than the

Lynsted

fabric without, was a hunting lodge of the Black Prince. At this time, I read, it was possessed by Lucas de Vienne with no mention of the Prince. But owners should know best, and it is a pleasant reflection that memories of the Black Prince mingle with more tangible reminders of

91

Provender

Rasputin, the Grand Duke Nicholas, the Cossacks and the Tzar of all the Russias.

A mere four miles from Provender, but how different from it, is Otterden Place. While the mansion is controlled by a mutual housing society, part of the buildings are retained by the old family, whose present representative bears the same names as the heir entitled when Hasted was writing his history. As so often happens, the people at Otterden Place claim that the main part of the building is earlier than the modern writer alleges, but perhaps the argument is only between the late eighteenth and early nineteenth centuries. There is no dispute that the older parts are Tudor; some Victorian extensions clash only slightly with the harmonious whole and the large plateau to the north is said to delimit the extent of the mansion before a large part was pulled down, for economy we must suppose, in the eighteenth century. Behind the building is a well hundreds of feet deep, with a vertical windlass, donkey-operated until mains water arrived.

But the great surprise of Otterden is the church. As many different adjectives and similes are used to express its unusual design as there are explanations of the reason for it. Although built in the middle of the eighteenth century it could well pass for a building of ten years ago. It is brick built with stone facings; an oblong box with everything in perfect repair. The brickwork is practically in new condition and the inside is more like that of one of the smarter London churches than one in the wilds of Kent. The floor level of an earlier building was retained on the north side so that the monuments on it need not be disturbed. The series of sculptures continued after the building of the new church and with everything immaculately preserved, the gleam of the colours and gilt are quite undimmed by time. These monuments have a deserved fame. Probably the most dramatic is that to Sir Justinian Lewin lying stiffly in his armour while the full-sized figure of his widow kneels in mourning with the little daughter pulling at her skirts. The convention of the seventeenth century sculptors, following on the practice of the brass engravers, was to include small figures in the design of sculptured tombs representing the children of the deceased, usually very numerous. Therefore a pathetic note is struck by the tomb of John Bunce on the wall opposite to that of Sir Justinian. His family is duly sculptured and it amounts to one tiny cradle with a baby in it. All this is in an outlandish spot that even with the aid of maps and advance study one may have difficulty in finding, which is simply typical of Kent.

The next parish, Throwley – the name rhymes with 'Cowley', not 'holy' – is noted for the family seat of

Charing High Street

Belmont, in the grounds of which is a golf course which, although no national championship has been held there, must be one of the most charming and delightful in the country to play on for sheer pleasure. The famous family of Sondes were seated in this parish for many generations until, in the time of Charles I, they moved over to

Sheldwich to build the great seat of Lees Court, which Inigo Jones is said to have designed.

Crossing the Faversham/Charing road we are now on the Challock plateau over which the old turnpike now calling itself the A252 leads from Charing to Chilham. Charing is not really on the Downs, though it gives its name to the hill which ascends them and from which a magnificent view of the Weald — with the quarry hills and Egerton church in the foreground — seems to stretch without limit, while on clear days the light and glare on the eastern horizon can only be the sea. The village itself is noteworthy for the set piece of the remains of the archbishop's palace, now converted to farm use, hard by the church.

Other villages on the shoulder of the Downs are Westwell, Eastwell and Boughton Aluph, three little beauty spots on the North Downs Way. Quiet little Westwell has an old watermill, complete if rusty, near the large church whose chancel is vaulted like a cathedral, and divided from the nave by tall pillars. At Eastwell the now ruined church and a deserted thirteenth-century house brood over the waters of the largest lake in Kent. At Boughton Aluph the walkway divides, the Canterbury spur going to the left down the Stour Valley, and the direct route to Folkestone and Dover to the right. Beyond the Stour we have the largest section of sheer unspoilt country remaining in Kent, the downland between the Canterbury–Dover and the Canterbury–Ashford roads bisected by the Roman Stone Street from Canterbury to Lympne. West of the Roman road are the uplands of Waltham, Hastingleigh and Elmsted, so familiar to Canterbury people and favourite spots for motoring, walking and riding, and giving more great views across the Weald and of the coast from Hythe to Beachy Head. There are no villages along the Stone Street; it runs straight and, from the point where it reaches the 400-foot contour until the escarpment, fairly flat. Eastwards two great valleys cut the Downs: the Elham Valley is watered by only the Nailbourne, a stream of intermittent flow, while the Alkham Valley, running from Hawkinge to Dover, has a rivulet a mile or so long at the Dover end. There are lesser valleys too, vales where woods and twisting lanes and ancient houses are thrown together haphazardly, as at Denton.

The quietest and most remote country of Kent is that between the Elham Valley and Stone Street; Palmstead, Bladbean, Farthingsole Farm – these names bring back memories of happy solitude under summer skies. There are even gated roads, and at Stelling a tract of unenclosed common survives as Stelling Minnis. "The inhabitants … are as wild, and in as rough a state as the country they dwell in", wrote the historian.

Beyond the Elham Valley the Kent Downs have a final fling, with the Paddlesworth–Acrise massif where they rise for the last time to the 600-foot contour. North-east of the Canterbury–Dover road the tilted slab that is the downland sinks gradually until sea-level is reached at Sandwich and Deal. On this gentle slope are the three remaining collieries of the small Kent coalfield – Snowdown, Tilmanstone and Betteshanger. The fourth pit – Chislet in the Stour Valley – has now been closed. There can be few coalfields that have fitted so unobtrusively into the rural landscape as that of Kent. Barfreston, for instance, is as quiet and as honestly rural as any village in the county, yet the pithead gear of Snowdown is little more than a mile away. The colliery at Betteshanger seems to have done nothing to mar the atmosphere of the little town of Eastry, once a residence of the kings of Kent, a bare two miles from the pithead, while Northbourne, one of the most interesting villages in Kent for those who know its history, survives with Betteshanger's pit workings almost on top of it.

Nearer to Dover, Waldershare Park has a large Queen Anne mansion, gutted and reconstructed about sixty years ago, and a grandiose eighteenth-century mausoleum for the personal glorification of its builder Sir Robert Furnese, whose monument in the church shows an equally self-confident approach.

95

Could there be any greater contrast to this consequentiality than the self-effacement of nearby Barfrestone? Because it has the best twelfth-century building in the kingdom Barfrestone does not need to advertise itself. The village is tiny; a church, a pub, a farm and half-a-dozen houses. Its name is an example of something you often meet with when you study Kent village names, a back-formation. In the eighteenth century the village was called, the name written, 'Barson'; Hasted mentions that it was anciently Barfriston and that it was written in the Domesday survey as Barfrestone. The name is now spoken and written as Barfreston, a compromise between the two old names (the pamphlet on sale in the church uses Barfreyston, but this does not seem to have caught on outside ecclesiastical circles). The reversion to an older name is of such common occurrence in Kent that one may ask whether, as a result of Hasted's researches, there was something of a general movement to resurrect the former names that had gone out of use. Barfreston hamlet and church are tightly confined in the descending curve of a narrow road; the only place for a car to stop seems to be on a few pathetic yards of tarmac by the inn, but this is clearly labelled "for customers only". The village is on the edge of the well-wooded area round the seat of Fredville, which, alas, is no more but beyond are the open fields of rolling downland stretching almost to the sea.

For nearly 300 years the parish has been noted for its healthiness. At a funeral in 1700 the minister resident in the parish was buried at the age of 96; the minister who preached the funeral sermon was 82, and the reader of the service 87; the parish clerk was of the same age, and the sexton 86. *Several* of the neighbouring parish of Coldred who attended were above 100 years old. So says Hasted, and we must believe him; unless perchance he had his notes mixed up and was actually reporting a meeting of the Barons of the Cinque Ports.

Barfreston church is unique; if there is any other that has kept unaltered its Norman structure I am afraid I have not seen it. It is quite a tiny place, and but for the excellent lighting would be rather gloomy inside with its slitty Norman windows and heavy Norman arches. It is the feeling of one architectural entity of great age that is attractive, especially when you have seen so many churches with one little piece Norman and the rest anything from thirteenth century to late Victorian. The outside is completely different from any other Kent church; the lower part is of flint with stone dressings, but the upper is of Norman ashlar work, with a wheel window of unusual design in the east gable, and sculpture wherever it can be worked in.

Barfreston church

The zenith of the sculptor's art at Barfreston, and the nadir of subject matter, are in the carving of the stonework surrounding the south doorway. The central figures of Jesus and an archbishop seem to the modern mind to be insulted and degraded by the two inner concentric rings of carvings on the voussoirs – or surrounds – many of which are symbolical of the Devil and all his works, and everything unclean. Outwardly, indeed, the figures are merely grotesque and unseemly in such a context: a monkey rides a goat; another ape blows the pipes of Pan; a bear plays the harp; a hare and a partridge have a drinking bout; and there are human scenes, stated to be heavily symbolical and a warning against the sins of the flesh. Perhaps, in this year of grace, we should just laugh; but for that central figure one might think we were meant to. As cleverly executed and with a seemlier theme are the vignettes on the third and outer of the concentric rings, which show mainly the people of the manor doing their various tasks, with but three religious subjects, not monkeys this time, but Elijah, John the Baptist and King David.

I do not pretend to understand the medieval mind; I only know that probably the strangest thing to be seen in Kent, at the same time one of the architectural marvels of England, is to be found in this village of a few hundred souls in a backwater near a Kentish coal pit.

Birling

CHAPTER SEVEN

Rivers of Mesopotamia

Kent is rich in archaeological sites of all periods from the Stone Age onwards, as we have already heard, but one can scarcely leave the subject at that. On the other hand, to explore the archaeology of Kent in depth (to use a fashionable expression) would require a complete book, if not an encyclopaedia. The best-known antiquities are not concentrated in any one part of the county, but are to be found far and wide, from the Iron Age fort at Oldbury to the Roman one at Richborough, from the roadside settlements at Springhead near Gravesend to the pharos on the cliffs of Dover.

No part of the county is richer than the Darent and Medway valleys, so perhaps, as a compromise, we may in this one chapter concentrate rather more on the past and its vestiges. It is to emphasize this approach that we have selected the heading of this chapter. The explanation is to be found in old Lambarde's pages, when he says apropros of Dartford: "Now be we returned into Mesopotamia, for so me thinketh that this countrie lying between the rivers of Darent and Medway may not unaptly be termed" – Darent being presumably the Tigris and Medway the Euphrates of Kent; Maidstone is, we assume, its Babylon – nice shooting, Mr Lambarde!

We can look first at two important groups of Stone Age megaliths without parallel in the southeastern part of Britain: Kit's Coty and Little Kit's Coty or the Countless Stones to the east of the Medway, and the Addington long barrow and Chestnuts (so called) and the Coldrum Stones to the west. The last are a mile or two from the river but they are all part of the same Neolithic burial area.

Kit's Coty House (a quite meaningless name) near Bluebell Hill on the road from Maidstone to Rochester is probably the most famous antiquity in Kent; it consists of the stone burial chamber of a former long barrow, a mound that was at least 180 feet in length and has disappeared completely through being ploughed over. Little Kit's Coty, otherwise the Countless Stones, about a quarter of a mile down the hill, is now accepted as being the remains of a much smaller D-shaped barrow, but the stones of its burial chamber are fallen, not erect like those at Kit's Coty. About four miles west is Addington which also has the remains of two megalithic monuments, the

Kit's Coty House

Coldrum is (to me) no less interesting to look at. It is on two levels: there is a kind of terrace, dominated by the main stones of the burial chamber on the upper level, with dramatic effect; then you can go up the steps at the side on to the higher level where the shape of the barrow is outlined by huge fallen stones, technically known as peristaliths. In the general area of Kit's Coty House the countryside is littered with sarsen stones, some having intriguing but invariably inaccurate names, such as the General's Tombstone, the Coffin Stones, and the White Horse Stone. Kit's Coty is more accessible than the Coldrum Stones, but to see both you have to walk some distance. It was most inconsiderate of the neolithic people to place their monuments so inconveniently. Such at least would be the view of a certain American visitor to Canterbury: he observed that it was typical of the British lack of business sense that one of the main attractions of the city, the Roman pavement, was located down an obscure lane and not in the main street.

The Neolithic age in Britain was the third millennium BC, and this dating ties in very well with that of the well-known Halling man, whose skeleton was dug up in 1912 near to the River Medway. The Second World War had a rejuvenating effect on this individual; he had been written off as being a relic of the Mesolithic period (pre-Neolithic) and his fossilized bones were sent to the

Addington long barrow and the 'Chestnuts', the remains of the burial chamber of another D-shaped barrow. Some mile to the north, but double that distance by road in the heart of the country on the southern face of the Downs, are the Coldrum Stones, which represent a square barrow. Though less well known than Kit's Coty,

100

Royal College of Surgeons in London. When this place was blown up in the Blitz, people said, "Well, that is the last of the Halling man." But his bones were recovered and tested anew, using modern techniques of radio-carbon dating, which showed that the gentleman was buried 4180 BP (give or take 190 years each way and understanding that the letters stand for Before the Present – 1969). He was therefore Neolithic and not Mesolithic; the war made him hundreds of years younger.

The lower Medway valley continued to be important in the Bronze and Iron Ages; it has produced gold ornaments and urn-fields dated to these respective periods.

When we come to the Roman era the floodgates, metaphorical ones of course, open. On the Darent, in addition to the famous Lullingstone, villas have been excavated at Darenth, Horton Kirby, Farningham, Shoreham and Otford; on the Medway Roman buildings of one sort or another have been uncovered at Teston, Barming, Eccles, Burham and Holborough. In the last case it was discovered that Holborough Knob, a well-known landmark in the valley, was in fact a Roman burial mound yielding rich and interesting finds. The Knob has, however, now disappeared from the landscape.

The Roman occupation lasted longer in Kent than anywhere else, as the fortress of Richborough was the first to be established and last to be evacuated. It is even thought by some people that twenty or thirty years after the Romans had evacuated Britain they returned and reoccupied Richborough for a year or two.

Kent saw the various ups and downs of the Roman period; things by no means remained static. Sometimes there was prosperity, then decay, then revival, and finally collapse. Nowhere can the vicissitudes be better studied than in the story of Lullingstone villa, which unlike most excavated sites has been roofed over and preserved.

The Saxons were not great builders, but from the time of the coming of the Normans, buildings of architectural interest are thickly spread in all directions; of the many hundreds of manor houses mentioned by Hasted I should say that the names of well over 50 per cent still survive. The Darent has a good sprinkling of them, and the Medway a vast array.

However it would be very academic for us to confine archaeology to its technical meaning. Even the Kent Archaeological Society does not attempt to do that, nor does its journal *Archaeologia Cantiana* – commonly called *Arch. Cant.* Once you get to that time in our history from which documents and books have survived, much of what we know about the period is learnt from written

101

sources, although here and there archaeology – that is digging – can still supply a few of the missing facts. I would certainly regard anything up to the Elizabethan period as coming within the sphere of the archaeologist for our present purposes; though we cannot attempt to investigate every medieval church; there are over 400 of these in the county and a goodly proportion of them are to be found in and around our two valleys.

The archaeologists, who delight in digging up the traces of past civilizations, cannot very well grumble if the Petroleum Age spreads its own strange installations over the landscape. Thousands of years hence our successors will uncover them with delight, and compose learned reports about them. At the same time we can take little pleasure in recording these changes. What are they?

In the eighteenth century the Medway valley was unspoilt. Here is a typical description of the view from East Barming: "an assemblage of objects on which nature and art appear to have lavished their choicest endeavours to form a scene teeming with whatever can make it desirable both for pleasure and profit." The River Medway "meanders its silver stream" now as it did then, but even on this stretch of the Medway industry has infiltrated here and there. To enter little Yalding, for instance, from the west, one has to go under a kind of triumphal arch of industrial piping. Elsewhere, Maidstone and Rochester have become large industrial towns, and Aylesford is ringed with factories but is itself unspoilt. The rot has now spread to places like Snodland and Cuxton.

On the Darent too the little villages have swollen to become dormitory suburbs and haunts of the industrial entrepreneur. But the beauty remains in stretches of that valley; one might (for a short time at least) be in Westmorland, and the Medway, above the market town of Tonbridge, waters some of Kent's and England's most famous beauty spots. But Penshurst and its delightful surroundings find a place with the other great seats in a later chapter.

Industrial though Maidstone and Rochester may be, I must say a word about them. Rochester, the Roman Durobrivae, has the cathedral and the castle that the great Bishop Gundulph built just after the Conquest, and anybody who reads Rochester's famous monastic book of words, the *Textus Roffensis*, knows that it is still stained with the waters of the River Thames from the time when a learned gentleman borrowed it and went to London on a barge that sank beneath him. Another great man was Bishop Fisher who helped Henry VIII to write for the Pope the anti-Reformation pamphlet that earned the King and his successors the title of Defenders of the

Faith, but who, when later he tried to defend it himself — against Henry's designs — lost his head.

Another famous tale of Rochester is that of the bridge. The present one is the third since Roman times. The conservators of Rochester bridge became a great and wealthy body, much esteemed for their success in creating order out of the medieval chaos when the repair of the different piers of the bridge was the feudal liability of this and that parish or manorial overlord. Today the Rochester Bridge Trust still carries on their useful work.

About Aylesford I can offer mainly historical gossip. In AD 455 tradition asserts that there was a battle fought here between the Britons and the Saxons which the Britons won. In this conflict Horsa, the brother of Hengist the Saxon chief, and Categern, brother of the British king, were both killed in single combat and were buried — Horsa at Horsted and Categern the Briton at Kit's Coty House, from whose names this village and megalith derive their own. As both the derivations are complete nonsense one wonders how true the story of the battle itself may be. Another semi-battle took place between King Edmund Ironside and the Danes in 1016. Edmund defeated the enemy at Otford and pursued them as far as Aylesford and was persuaded by treacherous advice to give up the pursuit. The holder of the manor of Aylesford in the reign of Henry III (John de Grey) was

responsible for a very revealing medieval fashion note. He so greatly gained the King's esteem that he "received at the royal hand a hood of white cloth embroidered with blue men dancing, buttoned before with great pearls." He also had accoutrements of Indian silk bestowed on him on which the arms of Sir Stephen de Cosyngton of Aylesford were painted.

Rochester Cathedral

About half a mile down the stream from the village of Aylesford is the collection of stone buildings known as the Friars. In the thirteenth century one of the first two houses of the Carmelites was founded here, but of their monastery the remains — the cloisters and parts of the refectory and of the prior's hall — are small in proportion to the modern rebuilding. The accretions range from the immediate post-Reformation period to the present time, for in 1949 the modern Carmelites took possession and created a great centre for pilgrimage with a new church, open sanctuary and chapels richly decorated with ceramics and wood sculpture.

Allington Castle is on the Medway between Maidstone and Aylesford. The Carmelites who seem to have taken this stretch of the Medway under their wing are in occupation of this imposing medieval stone castle. The gravel extraction works at the entrance to the grounds may dampen the spirits, and the boating marina (Marina di Maidstone presumably) just downstream from the castle at least prevents the more romantically minded from being completely lost in medieval visions. It is true that a good deal of restoration did take place in the first quarter of the present century, but Allington is in no sense a fake; it dates from the reign of Edward I but rose prominently into history in the sixteenth century, first as the home of the poet Sir Thomas Wyatt and then that of his son of the same name who led the rebellion against Mary Tudor in 1554 with fatal results to himself and to many of his adherents.

Maidstone, next on our itinerary, has its archbishop's palace and its All Saints' church, its Corpus Christi Hall, and some other medieval buildings. There is a playground that was once Penenden Heath, the meeting place for the Shire, and a public park that is still called the Mote, after the ancient seat of the Romney family.

Above Maidstone the Tonbridge road passes through Barming, and then enters on a stretch of the valley where, for an instant, one may look on a scene which has changed little since Hasted eulogized it. Works of man that pleased him, the medieval Teston bridge and the seat of Barham Court, are marred only slightly by the railway. Teston itself is bitty and modern; Wateringbury has an obtrusive railway station and a prominent brewery, but its church, slate roofed and gloomy in its interior, has an object (which we hope is genuine) of the greatest interest, the Dumb Borsholder of Chart. The Borsholder was a sort of parish constable and needless to say they were usually people, but fifteen houses in the Wateringbury area were governed by this Dumb Borsholder, a wooden stake with a spike at one end and sundry iron rings at the top and along its sides. A man was always elected to be the deputy of the Dumb

Maidstone, Palace and Medway

Borsholder and it was the deputy who pocketed the yearly fee of one penny from each of fifteen houses in the liberty payable to the Borsholder. This remarkable object is now secured to the wall over the entrance door of Wateringbury church.

Next on the Medway tour is Mereworth. Is it true, as a very distinguished Kent authority has said, that it is pronounced 'Meerworth'? The reply I received when I enquired for 'Meerworth' was that no such place was known in the neighbourhood. Mereworth Castle, like so many castles in Kent, is really nothing of the sort; it is strictly Mereworth House built in the eighteenth century by the Earl of Westmorland copying a Palladian villa at Vicenza. The church and vicarage which stood in the way of this grandiose plan were swept away and rebuilt half a mile away. The passer-by on the main road who merely gives Mereworth church a casual glance perhaps notices only that it is somewhat more ornate than the average Kent church, but on a closer look and even more on going inside one receives the impression of an eighteenth-century version of a Roman basilica, quite different from anything else in the county.

At West Peckham there is a charming little church with a Saxon tower overlooking the village green and the pub. Inside the church has a sort of retiring room with Hepplewhite chairs for the squire, reached by a flight

Mereworth Castle

of steps from the body of the church.

To continue the tour of the Medway valley, cross the river on a byroad and make for Tudeley. A big pile of buildings will appear on the skyline to the right, Somerhill, the great residence built in the reign of Queen Elizabeth by Richard Burgh, Earl of Clanrickard. Of him it is related that he had a striking resemblance to the late Earl of Essex, so much so that Queen Elizabeth tried to make advances to him.

As we often say, Kent has always something up its sleeve and in the little, not very ancient, church of Tudeley is a masterpiece of stained glass, its composition said to resemble a water-colour painting, by Marc Chagall.

The last stop before turning for Tonbridge is Capel. It is very quiet and sheep often graze in the churchyard, but the little Norman church is a gallery of art of medieval wall-paintings restored by Professor Tristram.

The ancient history of Tonbridge centres round the adventures of the medieval castle. As built by the Normans, it consisted of a motte and bailey, the former an earthen mound on which a keep was later constructed. Of the keep, foundations only remain, but the motte itself, of impressive height and steepness, survives. The bailey (the encircling walls), though reduced in the main to foundations or a mere core, can be traced for the full circuit, with one side protected by the waters of the Medway. About 1300, styles in castle building changed, and the lords of Tonbridge abandoned the keep in favour of the colossal gatehouse that can be seen today, complete but for roof, battlements and internal structures; in 1300 all activities, military and domestic, were concentrated on this new edifice which had thick walls, portcullis and arrow slits for the former and, upstairs, a large living-hall (55 feet by 29) for the latter.

The tale of Tonbridge Castle is lurid. Its ancient stones have been lit with the flickering flames of England's internal disputes, domestic and religious quarrels, plottings and usurpations from the time of the Conquest. In Domesday there is no description of Tonbridge, but we know it was possessed by Richard de Tonebridge, lord of the Lowy, a district round the town. Richard, also called FitzGilbert, was descended from the first Duke Richard of Normandy; he acquired the town and the castle towards the end of the Conqueror's reign in exchange for Brionne in Normandy. There is a curious story that to make sure that the swop should be a fair one, men went to Normandy and carried a rope round the whole extent of Brionne, then brought the rope back to England and with it measured out a corresponding area round Tonbridge. The castle was no mere ornamental residence, for its owners had to put up with siege after siege beginning with Richard himself who supported Robert Curthose against William Rufus but was forced to surrender and give allegiance to the red-headed king. His eldest son Gilbert also rebelled against

107

Rufus with the same unsatisfactory result. The Tonebridge's took the name Clare and later married into the Earldom of Gloucester, which seems to have encouraged them to try their luck once more. Again they rebelled, this time against King John, again were besieged and again had to give in. The lords of Tonbridge were in the field once more in the reign of Henry III; the then Earl of Gloucester left the defence of the castle to his wife, it was besieged and she was captured. Continuing the tale of woe, another Earl, Gilbert de Clare, being captain of the vanguard of the King's army in Scotland, was slain in the battle of Bannockburn. His inheritance was partitioned and Tonbridge was allotted to Hugh de Audley in the right of his wife. He quickly fell into the family customs and confederated with discontented barons so that King Edward II again seized the castle. We then get an array of well-known Kentish names appearing on the record: the King committed the castle to Bartholomew de Badlesmere who rebelled so that Edward gave the castle to Henry de Cobham, but his deputy, of the name of Crevequer conspired against the King who ordered the castle to be demolished and Crevequer hanged; only the second instruction was, however, carried out. A later lord of Tonbridge was Ralph, Lord Stafford, who commanded the van of the army of the Black Prince at the battle of Crécy. In the fifteenth century the Staffords became Dukes of Buckingham for services rendered and a couple of them were slain fighting for the Lancastrians in the Wars of the Roses; nevertheless one of their descendants, Henry Duke of Buckingham, became one of the chief confidants of the Yorkist Richard III who loaded him with honours and possessions. But family traditions could not be denied and Henry was soon in arms leading a Welsh army against Richard. At this stage we hear the unedifying story of the treachery of Ralph Bannister. The River Severn was in flood and the Welshmen without food or money decided to go home, leaving the Duke stranded. He took refuge in the house of his old servant Bannister not far from Shrewsbury but the wily King Richard having offered a reward of £1,000 for the discovery of the Duke, Bannister betrayed him to the Sheriff of Yorkshire who apprehended the fugitive "dressed in a piled black cloak" in a grove near Bannister's house and conveyed him to Salisbury where he was, on the following day, without arraignment or judgment, beheaded in the open market place. His son Edward was given back all his father's estates but was unwise enough to be uncivil to Cardinal Wolsey – Henry VIII was now on the throne. This resulted in a charge of high treason and a beheading on Tower Hill. All in all it does seem that Tonbridge was not exactly a nice peaceful place to inherit. No more was the manor of Southborough, another of the late Duke's possessions which Henry VIII conferred on Sir Thomas More, who, as is well known, became Lord Chancellor, refused to sign the oath of supremacy and was also executed on Tower Hill. Canterburians especially remember that his head was set on London Bridge for a time but then brought to the city by his daughter Margaret Roper, and deposited in the vault of St Dunstan's church.

We are even now not finished with the record of blood. The next owner of the manor was George Bullen, Viscount Rochford, son of Thomas Earl of Wiltshier and Ormond, and brother of Queen Anne Boleyn. When Henry VIII wanted to be rid of Anne one of the charges against her was that of incest with her brother, who was found guilty of high treason and beheaded. The Crown then granted the manor of Southborough to John Dudley, Earl of Warwick, but he hurriedly exchanged it with the King for other premises. In the reign of Queen Elizabeth it was in possession of Sir Richard Sackvyle, who, after some years, sold it to another well-known Kent character, Thomas Smith of Westenhanger, commonly called Customer Smith because he made his money by farming the customs of London and the county did not wish him to forget this fact. The manor

Tonbridge, Chequers

of Tonbridge had also in the seventeenth century come into commercial hands and presumably these gentlemen were too busy with their financial affairs to have time to plot against the kings and queens, so that, except for a brief interruption during the Civil War when the castle's interior was dismantled on the order of Parliament, peace has reigned at Tonbridge ever since. As Dr Johnson remarked: "there are few ways in which a man can be more innocently employed than in getting money."

In the sixteenth century Sir Andrew Judde founded a free grammar school which developed into the present public school. Less well known is its offshoot, the Judde School for local boys. It seems that they were 'hived off' from the other school in Victorian times.

Compared with the Medway, which is by far the greatest river of Kent, the Darent is but a small stream. The little river rises near Westerham, but as it flows from thence through Brasted and Sundridge it is little more than a ditch, the river recognizable as such starting in the Otford–Sevenoaks neighbourhood, and cutting through the Downs in a valley where it has to rub shoulders with a very busy main road and for several miles with a railway as well. It enters the Thames at Dartford, the ford over the Darent, now an industrial town, but made famous in history as the place where Wat Tyler's revolt began with a murderous assault by that gentleman on one of the collectors of the poll tax. Not that industry is new in Dartford. In Elizabeth's reign, Lambarde wrote:

Upon this Darent also, have beene lately erected two Milles of rare devise (or rather singular, within our Realme) the one emploied for the making of all sortes of Paper: the other exercised for the drawing of Iron into Wyres, and bigger lengthes and fashions, as well for the readier making of Nailes of all kindes, as for the easier dispatch of Barres for windowes, and other Services.

Above Dartford the first village is Darenth. The church there is a typical Kent flint church with its hotchpotch of architecture going back earlier than most, to the Saxon. Hard by a busy road and pressed by a dusty builders' yard, it is in an equivocal neighbourhood typical of this area. To emphasize the point, the moderns have built on to the Norman church a brick and glass single-pitched parish room of no-nonsense modern style. This church is probably the only one in Kent with Saxon features and modern wash-basins.

Working upstream again after a couple of miles you come to Sutton-at-Hone, not an attractive village and made less so by the heavy traffic, but having one oasis of peace, the estate of St John of Jerusalem. Now in the custody of the National Trust, it was once a commandery of the Knights Hospitaller and centuries later the residence of Edward Hasted, the historian of Kent, who transformed and reconstructed it in what he would doubtless have called the modern taste. The church provides another oasis to visit. The fact that it is kept locked may not be entirely due to the vandalistic pretentions of the modern English for in 1615 the building was seriously damaged by a fire caused by a person discharging a gun in the church at a bird.

The church at Horton Kirby is unattractive externally, spoilt by a brick tower, but nearby Farningham is an excellent place for lunch and shopping for simple wants. The river crossing with an old ford and mellow hostelry adjoining, the elegant and picturesque mill house, the fine old church set amidst Georgian buildings, justify the wisdom of those who arranged to carry the A20 road round Farningham on a bypass

Farningham charms the tourists rather than the archaeologists, to whom Eynsford a mile further on, and its neighbourhood, beckon. The twelfth-century castle cared for by the Department of the Environment, as we must now call them, is not very exciting. A featureless curtain wall surrounds foundations of the hall and other buildings within. Now comes the famous Eynsford view seen on many a calendar and tourist handbook, of the ford, the humped-back bridge, and the timbered buildings beyond, made more interesting by the hidden knowledge that the road leads to the Roman villa of Lullingstone. The church is as old as Darenth but bigger and more pleasant in its setting. The de Bosviles are buried there.

Eynsford

At the villa everything is well organized, with different parks for buses and private cars; a large shed encloses the remains. Inside the catwalks for viewing are on two levels: from the lower, one sees a meaningless jumble of walls but on the upper stage from a birdseye view of the whole the plan becames apparent with the eye-catching tessellated pavements in the centre.

111

I have kept Lullingstone until nearly the last because the remains of the Roman villa are one of the renowned sights, not just of Kent, but of Britain. It was discovered in 1939 when two people detected a Roman wall under the roots of a fallen tree. Because the Romans used tessellated pavements where we would use Wilton carpets, we have here inherited from them two large and richly ornamented pavements on which Europa is seen carried away by the bull and the hero Bellerophon, riding the winged horse Pegasus, spears the monster Chimera, in fable a cross between a lion and a serpent, but here looking more like a pussycat. Pre-Nazi swastikas and Latin hexameters add to the decorative scheme. Christian relics, marble busts and painted plaster pictures heighten Lullingstone's appeal. Needless to say, the archaeologists have got busy on the subject of Lullingstone with lengthy technical reports, but these are mostly for their own instruction rather than the entertainment of the public who, if they want to find out about Lullingstone, had best see it; that is what it is there for.

That we have to concentrate so much on archaeology is the only excuse we can have for passing by the noble seats of the Franks, near Horton Kirby, and Lullingstone Castle. And to finish the Darent valley we must press on to Shoreham, Otford and Kemsing. The first is delightful but unassuming with its atmosphere of riverside charm.

Before Otford the road traverses a mile or more of suburban ribbon development; then of a sudden comes a meeting of roads, a roundabout and a swift glimpse of the remains of the archbishop's palace. We must drive on and park, and walk back, or leave it for some other time as we cannot even stop to look at it. It is a massive chunk of Tudor brickwork still standing three storeys high, but only a tiny fragment of the huge palace built by Archbishop Warham in Henry VIII's reign, "minding to leave to posteritie some glorious monument of his wordly wealth and misbegotten treasure." I leave that last word to Lambarde.

At Kemsing you would expect Lambarde to be quite popular. After all, he wrote the letter of dedication of his masterpiece from St Clere's a mile away to the east, and included Kemsing in the somewhat arbitrarily selected list of the places of which he gave an account. But the learned ones of Kemsing have but a lukewarm admiration for the amiable William; he printed a good story about the image of St Edith, telling how the priests lined their pockets by exploiting its allegedly miraculous powers, but after mentioning this circumstance, instead of describing the image, or its exact site, or even Kemsing itself (which would have been most acceptable), Lambarde preferred to plunge into one of his religious diatribes, attacking polytheism, popery, superstition, idolatry and so forth, but leaving guessing the students of Kemsing's past.

In the middle of the fifteenth century, at the time of Jack Cade's rebellion (which the people of Sevenoaks proudly claim to have originated in their town), the manor of Kemsing was held by James, Lord Say and Sele, who was murdered by the London mob at the instigation of the rebel, one of his alleged crimes being the release of Anjou and the delivery of Maine to the French. With him was beheaded his son-in-law William Cromer of Tunstall, who was at that time sheriff of Kent. Cromer was avenged when Alexander Iden of Westwell, his successor as sheriff, in turn slew Cade, to receive a reward of a thousand marks from the King, and the hand of Elizabeth, widow of Cromer and daughter of Lord Say. What a plot for a Hollywood Wild West epic! Shakespeare partly used it in *Henry VI* (*Part II*) but would surely have developed it further if he had been reared on the same diet as modern television-watchers and cinema-goers. This may be a digression from the subject of Kemsing, but it is typical of the rich texture of Kentish history that strands from Kemsing, Tunstall, Westwell, Sevenoaks, Cheapside, Maine and Anjou are woven into this one small part of its fabric. We read, too, that George Bullen (or Boleyn), the brother of Anne, later held the manor here – linking its history

with the more lurid episodes in that of Hever Castle.

Commentators and guidebook writers are apt to speak somewhat patronisingly of Kemsing because it is in what they term "commuter country", but approaching from the east (does one *have* to come from the London direction?) you see nothing of this. Yaldham Manor, St Clere, Heaverham, Crowdleham are all strung out in open country at the foot of the Downs. At Kemsing one finds, as the road dips and curves, a typical Kentish village; surveying the small village green with the well of St Edith, its head shaped like an enormous keyhole, one notices that there is not a single commuter dwelling in sight in any direction, unless one counts the 1906 vintage Hildenborough Hall, unkindly nicknamed 'Treacle Towers', high up on the escarpment.

The attractive church offers many things worth seeing, most notably a roundel of thirteenth-century stained glass, looking stylistically much more ancient than the twelfth- and thirteenth-century glass in Canterbury Cathedral. St Mary's has also a splendid funerary brass which, in the dim light, can easily fool the visitor into thinking that it is what it is not. The large figure of a robed man has below it the usual Gothic lettering, on reading which one is surprised to find the date 1906. Moving so that the light falls better on the incised lines one sees the figure of a modern-looking gentleman: the

113

memorial is in fact for a vicar who died in the year above-mentioned.

Near the village green is the Box House, supposedly on the site of the convent where St Edith was *born*, while St Edith Hall, a short distance away, is claimed to be the finest village hall in Kent, with hopscotch court at the front and a pile of beer-kegs at the back.

From Kemsing you can take a byroad through the quiet woods to Oldbury Hill and Ightham, again without seeing commuters.

Kemsing and Canterbury have much in common, in particular a great past and a prosperous present, a conjunction which is anathema to the self-styled 'conservationist'. Ancient places, according to this English brand of 'le snobbisme', are there for the tourist to gape at and the conservationist to drool over, not to be lived in nor to thrive prosperously!

Kemsing church

CHAPTER EIGHT

The Gentle Stour

It is probable that there never were many other incumbents, in Kent or elsewhere, like James Croft, the Saltwood pluralist, and it is certain that there are none today. Those who are not too closely involved in church affairs may, at the same time, have an image of the typical country parson as a man with a pleasant and fairly easy job for which he is, however, rather badly paid. Clergymen do not, of course, conform to any one type, any more than do we laymen in our various walks of life, but in reality the usual picture in country parishes is that of a man kept busy morning till night – taking services, writing sermons, visiting, organizing and administering. The same may well be true in the town, but the circumstances are different and the country parson is a better known and more prominent figure than one in the town, and he will tell you that out in the villages you need more clergy in proportion to the population than in the cities.

As you travel round Kent you will find that many of the country parishes are linked, in pairs, less often in threes, and in one case, Romney Marsh, in a group of several parishes. You may put this down to declining congregations and lack of enthusiasm. There has undoubtedly been this falling off, but the real reason for the linkages is financial. The day of the dilettante parson, perhaps the youngest son of a moneyed family, is past and gone. Nowadays, to attract good men, however unmercenary, the Church must offer a worthwhile living for a worthwhile job, and to do this it must, in many cases, combine the resources of two parishes or more. There is a different picture when it comes to raising funds from the laity for parish causes. Even for quite expensive projects, such as building parish halls, I am told that the response from the single parish can be remarkably good. But let us get back to Kent, and the Kentish Stour in particular.

Although it is only a small river, the Stour has a surprisingly large watershed; with our minds on things ecclesiastical we may observe that, with its tributaries, it flows through seven of the sixteen rural deaneries of the diocese of Canterbury. The East Stour rises at Postling in the Elham deanery and the West Stour seventeen miles away at Lenham in that of Sutton. The others are East Bridge, West Bridge, Canterbury, East Charing and

North Lympne. The two branches of the river meet at Ashford.

The guidebook tells us that at Postling the East Stour issues from a leaden spout, though I confess I have not seen it; from the road the water, splashing and gurgling, can be heard but not seen. Every river must have its source somewhere, but very few churches have preserved their dedication stones as has St Mary's and St Radegund's in this village. It is a very small square of stone projecting from the wall behind the stalls on the north side of the chancel. The dedication of St Mary was made on the Feast of St Eusebius but the year is not given. Next to the churchyard is a farm with a huge grassy forstal or fold yard, completely surrounded by half-timbered stables and barns. The neat and spacious dignity seems reminiscent of Alsace rather than Kent.

From its source the East Stour, or, as some books call it, the Old Stour, wanders through the farmlands towards Stanford. Neither the church here, nor the village, is particularly interesting except for the ruins of the mansion of Westenhanger. I think these are amongst the most exciting and least appreciated of all the antiquities of Kent. When you read in the papers of racing 'at Folkestone' it really means at 'Westenhanger' – Folkestone is a good six or seven miles distant. The remains are tucked away behind the racecourse, and

though only a small fraction of the large and magnificent buildings that once existed, are still impressive. The Criol family, who were here in the reign of Edward I, probably built Westenhanger. In the time of Queen Elizabeth I its proprietor was none other than Thomas Smith, commonly called Customer Smith, whom we have heard about in the account of Tonbridge.

Some byways in the history of Westenhanger seem to anticipate by some hundreds of years the goings-on of our modern 'permissive society'. For instance, one of the towers still standing is said to be called Rosamund's Tower from the tradition that Henry II's lady friend was kept there for some time. The Criols died out and Westenhanger came eventually to the Poynings family, and when in the reign of Henry VIII Sir Edward Poynings died without legitimate issue there were four counterparts of the Fair Rosamund to come forward and offer for consideration the next best thing in the form of the fruits of their associations with the late Sir Edward. The eldest amongst this fourfold brood was created Sir Thomas Poynings and became quite a favourite of the Court, but he exchanged Westenhanger for other property. At its zenith the house had 176 rooms and 365 windows – it is amazing the number of medieval buildings that possessed this exact number either of rooms or of windows! – but in 1701 most of it was pulled down for the sake of the materials. A purchaser of it converted the remainder into a "small, neat edifice" for his residence, but this was again pulled down and an even smaller house built on the site of it, which we assume to be one that remains today; though in a dilapidated condition it is still a substantial Georgian house, built into part of the ruins. Nearly 200 years ago it was written that all that then remained were "the walls and two towers on the north and east sides of it which are yearly falling in huge masses into the adjoining moat; and the remaining ruins being covered with ivy and trees growing spontaneously on and through the sides of every part of them, exhibit an awful scene, and a melancholy remembrance of its antient grandeur." This is not a bad description of the scene that today greets anyone who is prepared to explain his presence to the employees of the racecourse company, penetrate past the buildings of the totalizator, skirt the silver ring and disregard the frames giving the numbers of the placed horses in the last race at the most recent meeting; and then make his way through a Malayan jungle of breast-high nettles and thorns. The poet who coined the expression "ivy-mantled tower" must surely have been at Westenhanger: where the house has been built into the ruins, mullioned windows overlook the moat and the circular medieval corner tower has been given a conical cap of Kentish tiles; round the corner the walls and towers are almost hidden in greenery. A farm enroaches upon the remains; in its yard Gothic doorways add dignity to the crumbling stonework of an extensive range of barns, under one of which, better built than the rest, the East Stour passes through an arch. It then meanders through open country towards Ashford and its meeting with the West Stour. Between the escarpment of the North Downs and the river there is a pleasant, gradually shelving country dotted with villages – Stowting, Brabourne, Brabourne Lees, Sellindge, Smeeth, Brook and Mersham. Hereabouts I sought for traces of the lost hundreds of Bircholt Franchise and Bircholt Barony, but found only a long lane, a straying cow, and a farmhouse with no pretensions whatever to ancient architecture.

In 1760 its then owner pulled down the ancient seat of Mersham-le-Hatch and began to build a new mansion which he did not live to finish; his architect was Robert Adam. But the great seat no longer houses the family who lived there from the time of Henry VII. They are still around but have retreated to a more modest dwelling in the parish, and sought a new role in the modern world; the Hatch now houses the Caldecott Community. This is the way to fight back, but how many of the great Kent families similarly survive? Where are the Deerings and Twysdens (or Twisdens), the Culpepers or

117

the Cobhams? Alas, they are as the snows of yester-year. Whether we should lament the disappearance of the wealthy patron of the parish or rejoice in the decay of a paternalism which clashes with modern ideas of self-styled democracy is a question to be answered.

Brabourne, Smeeth and Brook all have churches of

Brabourne church

solid Norman architecture and at Brabourne is a Norman window with the original twelfth-century glass still *in situ*, a rare phenomenon.* The family of Scott used this church for their burials although they lived at Scott's Hall (long disappeared) in the parish of Smeeth; they have left tombs and brasses and an interesting piece of sculpture, traditionally a shrine for the heart of John Baliol. The Scotts' family name was Baliol, but they dropped it in favour of one which merely showed their nationality, because they feared to give offence to Edward I who spent so much of his time disputing with Baliol the overlordship of Scotland.

St Mary's at Brook has a large and justly famous series of medieval wall paintings, restored many years ago by the well-known Professor Tristram, whose work at Capel we have already mentioned.

The stream that rises at Lenham is, in name at least, the River Stour itself and not a tributary. Today Lenham seems a lively enough little place with the court lodge, the church and the duck pond grouped prettily together, but in the eighteenth century it is described as being "dull and unfrequented, and of but little traffic". Happy days indeed, one would think, though the inhabitants, we are told, if asked if that was Lenham, would answer:

* I hear (1975) that it has been removed for cleaning!

"Ah, Sir; poor Lenham." Perhaps today they may answer the same but for the opposite reason; a place close by has been selected as a kind of marshalling yard for the TIR juggernaut container lorries passing to and from the Continent. There are even customs facilities.

Flowing through Chilston Park the Stour winds its way to Little Chart where the old narrow bridge carries the equally winding road from Charing to Pluckley near the ruins of the former Little Chart church. Distant from its village and with only a single farm within half a mile of it the church was nevertheless destroyed by a flying bomb. The little river seems deliberately to skirt round human settlements at Hothfield and Great Chart, and slips into Ashford by the back door, so to speak.

Three miles below the waters-meet at Ashford is the seventeenth-century bridge at Wye, which little town asserts with many voices, including those of history, religion and learning, its claim to some close attention. The church, built in the thirteenth century to succeed one mentioned in Domesday Book, was taken in hand by Archbishop Kempe (a scion of the local county family from the nearby seat of Olantigh, the founder of Wye College), and was restored by him. The chancel and transepts were beyond redemption in 1686 after the central tower fell down, and were rebuilt at the very beginning of the eighteenth century in the style of that

Lenham

time. Cardinal Archbishop John Kempe was the son of Thomas, younger brother of Sir Roger Kempe, whose ancestors had been settled at Olantigh for some generations. The archbishop was munificent in his works of charity, and in particular to the divinity schools, and to Merton College in Oxford. He founded and

119

bountifully endowed the college of Wye for the celebration of divine service and for the education of youth in the parish. When the college was suppressed, Henry VIII when granting its lands and possessions to Walter Butler made a proviso requiring Butler to provide and maintain a schoolmaster to teach the local boys in (Latin) grammar. When the said Butler neglected to carry out his side of the bargain his estate was forfeited. This was in the reign of Queen Elizabeth; both James I and Charles I concerned themselves in the matter and eventually the college was placed on a satisfactory footing with the aid of additional local benefactions. However, it fell on lean times and it was reconstituted as an agricultural college, affiliated to London University.

Downstream from Wye is Olantigh, the ancient home of the Kempes, and later of the Thornhills, one of whom, Major Thornhill, in 1711 fought a duel with Sir Cholmley Dering, Bart., in Tothill Fields, Westminster, in which Sir Cholmley received a wound of which he died the same day. The trustees sold Olantigh to the Sawbridges, the owners until the end of the eighteenth century. The old mansion was destroyed by fire in 1903 and the present building is accordingly Edwardian in its architectural flavour, but with some echo in general design of the earlier 1762 buildings.

120

Little Chart

Almost level with Olantigh on the left bank but a little distance from the river is another village whose church has been in the wars, literally − Boughton Aluph. It received quite small war damage, the effects of which spread with serious consequences, so much so that large-scale expensive renovations have been necessary. The quiet backwater of a village and its extension Boughton Lees on the Ashford–Faversham main road has some fine old buildings, sixteenth century and earlier.

Below Wye and Olantigh the Stour forces its way, as it has been put, through the Downs. The expression is a little misleading; it is probable that the river originally flowed northwards from the Downs and gradually ate its way further and further into them, until it joined up with another stream whose course was in the other direction, captured its headwaters and reversed its flow. The result is a narrow, twisting defile which is its most scenic stretch.

We have been hearing rather a lot about the clergy and their churches, but at Godmersham we have some relief from the ecclesiastical atmosphere in the shape of memories of Jane Austen. She was probably the most distinguished person connected with the parish since 822 when Beornulph, King of Mercia, gave it to Christchurch for the use of their refectory and clothing at the request of Archbishop Wlfred, L.S.A., which for the uninitiated means with the same privileges as Adisham, already given to that church.

At the beginning of the eighteenth century the manors in Godmersham known as Ford and Yallande were well and truly established in the hands of the family of Broadnax, one of whom, Thomas, got thoroughly bored with being so entitled and on inheriting the property of the May family he obtained an Act of Parliament in the thirteenth year of the reign of George I to change his name to May. Later on, "pursuant to the will of Mrs Elizabeth Knight, widow of Bulstrode Peachey Knight Esq.", Thomas decided again to change the family name, this time to Knight. When the affair came before Parliament for the second time an MP suggested passing an Act "for him to use whatever name he pleases". His son, Thomas Knight, left the place for life to his widow with the remainder to Edward Austen, of Rolling Place. The latter followed 'tradition' by changing his name to Knight. The eighteenth-century historian who reports these changes could not have anticipated the fame that the name of Austen would bring to Godmersham, for the lady novelist (sister of Edward) often stayed at Ford Place, or Godmersham Park as it is now called, and had a special bower (a predecessor, maybe, of Bernard Shaw's summer house) outside the house in which she wrote some of her novels, including perhaps *Mansfield Park* which is supposed to be a fictitious name for Ford Place or Godmersham Park. Eggarton Manor in this parish has a well-known feature, a donkey wheel.

Some space having been given to literature, ecclesiastical affairs must again claim attention because Godmersham's Norman church with its late Saxon tower

121

is specially interesting for two items if no others – the statue of Thomas Becket and the palimpsest brass. The statue, or more correctly bas-relief, was once fixed over the porch of the old hall of the manor house of Godmersham which was pulled down in the 1930s. The historian Hasted thought that it represented Prior Thomas Chillenden who, in Richard II's reign, made

Godmersham church

large additions and repairs to the manor house which was a favourite place of the priors of Canterbury. Now we are told it has been identified as a representation of Archbishop Thomas Becket and was executed not later than AD 1200. It originally decorated the end of a tomb; as one would expect, it is a somewhat crudely executed work though interesting in its detail – the ecclesiastical vestments and the impression of Canterbury Cathedral at the top.

It is not uncommon to hear of brasses that have been turned over and reused, and the display of them poses something of a problem. Sometimes the brass is kept secure in a locked vestry or elsewhere so that students may see both sides; sometimes after a rubbing has been made of the less good side, the brass is fixed so as to display the better one. At Godmersham one has the best of both worlds. The brass, dated 1471 and commemorating William Attilburgh, and Margaret his wife, and then reused in 1516 as a memorial to William Geffray, chantry-priest, is hinged to the south wall of the chancel so that the curious may read both sides.

In the village the old bridge, constructed in 1698, leads to the great house built in the Palladian style in 1732 with the aid of the May skekels. This, the vicarage and the church are all on a quiet wooded loop road from the busy A28.

Linked with Godmersham under the scheme I had already explained is Crundale. Its church has the old authentic atmosphere of Ten Commandments, Creed, Lord's Prayer and royal coat of arms and in a little chapel off the porch is an alabaster slab of the tomb of John Sprott, rector here, who died in 1466.

Hereabouts, scattered farmsteads are to be found, including Huntstreet which its owners know by its Saxon name of Cake's Yoke. Beneath the sixteenth-century building is an allegedly Saxon crypt comprehensively fitted out as a bar by the younger members of the family. The hills round here are the steepest in Kent, reminiscent of sub-Alpine Switzerland, and many are marked with lynchets – outlines of the prehistoric field system.

The scenic section of the Stour valley comes to its climax at Chilham. Here the old turnpike from the top of Charing Hill debouches from a side valley and joins up with the Canterbury–Ashford road, and on the tree-crowned bluff between the two valleys stand the village, the church and the castle. The river divides to serve a mill; beyond it are the hanging banks of Julliberrie Downs, so called after a fabulous giant supposed to be buried in what is really a long barrow. The history of Chilham Castle is rather like that of Tonbridge but without the sieges. In the Conqueror's time Fulbert had it as a subordinate of Odo of Bayeux; he stepped into his master's shoes (at Chilham at any rate) when the latter was disgraced. By making Fulbert his tenant in chief the Conqueror created the barony and honour of Chilham. Fulbert had to assume the burden of finding soldiers to help defend Dover Castle, and he and his family adopted Dover as their surname. Things began to get complicated for the Dovers in the reign of King John, whom they entertained as house guest while he carried on his argument with Archbishop Stephen Langton on the subject of Magna Carta. Then the family found itself without issue in the male line and Chilham went to the Earl of Athol, who was some sort of primitive Scotch Nationalist. King Edward I, who regarded himself as Overlord of Scotland and had no particular enthusiasm for devolution, seized Athol and had him attainted, and hanged on a fifty-foot high gibbet as a prelude to decapitation and burning. His forfeited lands including Chilham were granted to a well-known Kent character, the rich Lord Badlesmere of Leeds, who also came to a sticky end. A plotter against Edward II, he had to show his hand when Queen Isabella, with a suspiciously long train of armed attendants, demanded board and lodging for the night at Leeds. Bartholomew refused to let her in and so was attainted and beheaded. Perhaps intending to show that he was not such a bad sort, Edward then let

123

the sons of the two traitorous proprietors of Chilham enjoy its revenues in turn, but for life only. Eventually the lands were granted to Lord Roos, but one of his descendants found himself on the losing side in the Wars of the Roses. Henry VIII towards the end of his reign granted Chilham to Sir Thomas Chene (or Cheney), Treasurer of his Household and Warden of the Cinque Ports. Unluckily for Chilham he also had a manor, which he preferred, at Shurland on the Isle of Sheppey and he pulled down the greatest part of his seat at Chilham and used the materials to complete the great mansion of Shurland of which the ruins can be seen today; fortunately he spared the octagonal Norman keep and its curtain wall. This man's son sold Chilham to Sir Thomas Kempe whose family eventually resold to Sir Dudley Digges, a character well known in the history of the village, because he pulled down still more of the old mansion and built the present castle — red brick with sandstone trimmings — which was finished in the year 1616. Some writers attribute its design to Inigo Jones but not, it is thought, on any evidence other than the date of construction. Sir Dudley was a great man for sepulchral memorials and curious legacies and he it was who established the Digges foot race, a competition for young men and maids of Chilham and Sheldwich, the finals being run at Old Wives Lees for ten pound prizes, big money in those days. Since then the castle has changed hands many times.

Between the castle, which has had sundry facelifts both in the nineteenth and the present centuries, and the church, is a village square of great charm with many ancient timbered buildings, to which the tall trees half hiding the church make a wonderful backcloth, making one almost forget the disfigurement of the double line of motor cars which, as seems invariable in beauty spots, clutter up the centre of the square.

White palings surround the churchyard where the octagonal faced clock on the church tower peers over the yews. The tower's checkered pattern of alternate flint and stone is a typical Tudor feature and fits in with the evidence of a sixteenth-century will leaving money to build it. St Mary's is a big church; the nave and transepts are earlier than the tower, but the chancel is nineteenth century. It has many well-known monuments, some of which are unique in the use of Bethersden marble carved in such a way as to have a striking effect, similar to that of embossed upholstery. The tomb of Lady Margaret Palmer is so decorated, and also that of one of the Fogges. Lacking this unique quality, but more grandiose and spectacular, is the tomb of Lady Mary Digges who died in 1631. It has the well-known and often pictured figures of Justice, Prudence, Temperance and Fortitude

Chilham square

sitting round a pillar, probably inspired by Inigo Jones. As famous in his day as Jones was Sir Francis Chantrey, the nineteenth-century sculptor; he has a major work in this church, the monument to James Wildman who died, as we see, in 1816. Three mourning figures surround the tomb which bears the dead man's portrait in relief.

A short distance below Chilham we meet the city limits of the new expanded Canterbury. We will not anticipate its description, but leapfrog over it to where the tidal reaches of the Stour lie half hidden in the marshes where formerly the Wantsum flowed.

First, however, I owe an apology to the villages of Elham and Lyminge if I have given the impression that I intended to omit them. Near the last-named rises the Nailbourne, an intermittent stream that flows, so it is said, only when victuals are expensive and scarce; why it is not flowing at the present time (1974) no one can explain.* This unpredictable watercourse, when it does condescend to function, discharges into the Lesser and thence into the Great Stour, and so comes within my brief. The fine open valley, curving gently from Lyminge down to Barham and from thence to Bridge, has no permanent stream to give it a name and is therefore called after one of its charming villages – the Elham valley.

* It is now (1975) flowing and overflowing!

126

Elham's High Street is wide enough to give a good setting to the seventeenth-century building with elaborately carved timbers called the Abbot's Fireside. A short connecting road leads downhill to the Square, a quiet retreat with old houses on three sides and the churchyard on the fourth. Although the fabric of the church has twelfth-century origins, most of its interest is in the fixtures and fittings – sanctuary pavement, panelling, altar rail, reredos, organ casing and other woodwork. Most are twentieth century, but have some of the old materials reused. There is a stained glass window, too, that is modern but curious. Designed by the brother of a vicar, it displays the features of well-known Victorian characters in symbolic roles – Saul is 'played' by Thomas Carlyle, Samuel by Lord Salisbury, while Gladstone and Disraeli have walk-on parts. The *boy* David, Madame Patti impersonates while the hirsute *man* has the features of Walter Wodehouse – the Vicar!

The paradox of the large village, or small town, of Lyminge is that the church is better and the town itself worse than any other for miles around. The church has a history going back to the earliest days of Christianity in England. It is dedicated to St Mary and to St Ethelburga, the last-named being the daughter of King Ethelbert under whose reign the kingdom of Kent was converted by St Augustine. With Bishop Paulinus, the holy woman founded an abbey here for men and women and it is thought that the present building has part of the fabric of the original abbey church in its walling. In the study of ecclesiastical architecture, Lyminge is of the highest importance, as it is one of the small group of seventh-century churches whose plans are known. A recess in the church is generally supposed to have been the tomb of St Mildred – she founded the abbey at Minster-in-Thanet; Ethelburga succeeded St Mildred at Minster and both their bodies were brought to Lyminge.

The nave and chancel are Saxon, but the tower and north aisle are later. A stranger brought into this church without knowing its story would surely receive an instinctive impression of its venerability; it has the aura of a primitive cathedral. One can forgive Lyminge for its dearth of other attractions.

Having done tardy justice to Elham and Lyminge I can now o'erleap the widely spread new Canterbury and come to earth somewhere near the elegantly named Pluck's Gutter, where the waters of the Great and Lesser Stour, and the even lesser Wantsum, are finally united. The nearest villages are still called East and West Stourmouth, although the Stour has now to pursue a course of many miles to catch up with the fugitive sea. Parish names are not altered lightly, and no one would dream of changing them because of a little thing like the shrinking of the Wantsum from an arm of the sea into a minor land drain.

On the Canterbury–Sandwich road, to the south of the river's course, are two important villages, Wingham and Ash. Edward Hasted describes Wingham as a "village or town". It has an advantage over Chilham in its more tangible Roman connections; a large villa has been excavated and re-excavated a short distance from where the road from Canterbury enters the town–village. The church is also at this end, and opposite are the old canons' houses for the church was once collegiate, having a provost and six canons attached to it, as ordained by Archbishop Peckham in the 1280s.

The Canterbury road has the old college buildings and other fine houses; it turns at right angles to become the village high street in which there are many buildings of the sixteenth, seventeenth and eighteenth centuries. With a tree-lined street and parking restricted Wingham presents a fine bit of the old Kent. It has been no Tonbridge or even Chilham in producing rebels and so-called traitors. The best and worst it can show are three guidebook characters, one a very highly-connected nun, Elizabeth, daughter of the Marquis of Juliers, who broke her vows and ran off to get married; one (fictitious) associate of Jack Cade who found himself in one of Shakespeare's plays; and a favourite son who helped the

127

South Americans to rebel against Spain.

Until Cranmer gave it back to Henry VIII, along with so much other valuable property, the manor of Wingham belonged to the See of Canterbury. The Crown gave it to the Oxenden family, whose magnificent black and white marble monument stands in the church in the Dene chapel, named after the family seat. The arches between nave and south aisles are supported on wooden pillars. We read that the reason for his shoddiness is that in the sixteenth century the money subscribed for building stone pillars was embezzled by one Ffoggarde, a brewer. When the college was suppressed at the Reformation the big house belonging to it was given to the Palmer family, who also have their monuments in the church.

The end of the journey is now in sight, at Ash, last village of note near the Stour. Do not yet succumb to the fatigue of tramping round so many churches; Ash will revive your interest, because it has the finest array of tomb sculptures of any parish church in Kent, and a selection of brasses second only to Cobham. When last I visited St Nicholas's it was on a weekday, late in the afternoon and out of season for visitors. Yet there were people in the church, an American student making a rubbing of the Keriell brass, and a number of village children who were rushing about and shouting. After I had remonstrated with the youngsters, two English visitors came in and were looking at the monument of Sir Thomas Septvans and his wife and commenting on the line of kneeling children, some sculptured with skulls in their hands. One of the noisy children could be heard explaining to the strangers that those were the children who died before their parents. The children of Ash may be (some of them) rowdy, but there are no flies on them. On her brass, Jane Keriell, who died in 1455, is shown wearing a kirtle and a gown with very full sleeves, and most striking of all, a head-dress in the shape of a horseshoe with the ends upward, giving the effect of a pair of horns superimposed on a stylish-looking turban. Below are some verses beseeching the passer-by to pray for her soul. There are many monuments and tombs older than the Septvans monument that I have mentioned, effigies of knights and ladies some as early as the fourteenth century. Unfortunately the identities of the older ones are uncertain.

To end, perhaps a breath of fresh air would not come amiss. A sharp walk of about half a mile from the village will take us to Chequer Court, an ancient moated farmhouse and former manor. Further on, the lane takes you to the oddly named hamlet of Paramour Street, and from thence either to Westmarsh, Elmstone and Preston or to the marshes of the Stour flowing quietly on the last few miles of its course towards Sandwich and the sea.

CHAPTER NINE

Liberated, But Not Loose

One of the less reputable tales of Kentish folklore is the indelicate jest about the Women's Institute in Loose. The story runs like this: In all other villages of Kent, the Institute, if there is one, is entitled the so-and-so Women's Institute, but exceptionally, at Loose, to avoid misunderstanding, it is called 'The Women's Institute, Loose'. This is a joke on paper only; if spoken, it has no point because Loose is pronounced 'Looze'. This little place, on the outskirts of Maidstone, is in the Quarry Hills.

It is a shame to mock the Women's Institutes; the idea behind them – like that of the British Legion and the Two Minutes' Silence – came from North America, but by now they are thoroughly acclimatized over here. They have done wonders in improving the quality of life of countrywomen: they do not spend their whole time jam-making and fruit bottling, as some people seem to think; one of the organizers tells me that they are keen on the environment and local history, and try to educate themselves not just in cookery, gardening and handicrafts, but in music, drama, local government, public questions, and even international affairs. There are half a million women in the movement, and in Kent they have half an hour on Radio Medway each week.

And now, having made my peace with these Fair Maids of Kent, I suppose I must 'get on with the job' of saying something about these hills, sand hills, quarry hills, greensand ridge, green hills, stone hills, or whatever you like to call them. I will settle for 'quarry hills'. The origin of this subsidiary ridge between Downs and Weald we have already considered in some detail. They are unmistakable round Sevenoaks, and again in Boughton Monchelsea parish, south of Maidstone. Eastwards from the other Boughton, Boughton Malherbe, they gradually become less obvious until, at Great Chart, there is nothing more than a modest slope in the village street. At Aldington they reappear and carry on through Hythe to Folkestone, a country already familiar to us from earlier chapters.

The vale between the Downs and the quarry hills (sometimes called Holmesdale) seems to be nobody's child, so we can include that as well; this really means Trottiscliffe and Birling. Something has already been

Loose

neither one thing nor the other. I suppose the common denominator of the villages on the quarry hills is the use of the stone – in walls along the roads, in the fabric of churches, and for building generally.

In olden times, Boughton Monchelsea was the great place for quarrying, and it was from here that the stone was taken to build the Tower of London, and nearer home, the Westgate at Canterbury. It is very hard and brittle for a building stone, and I have been told that it is almost impossible to carve it because as soon as a mason gets to work with his hammer and chisel, chunks will simply fly off. 'Observing' the churches – you will recall that distinction between seeing and observing – you will notice that on the Downs their walls and towers are of flint, and on our quarry hills of ragstone, while away over in the High Weald, where they have another, different range of 'quarry hills', really the Hastings beds, buildings are of sandstone.

Coming back to our villages, you might think that the 'towniest' places would be those nearest to London, but this is not so. Rather than London, it is Maidstone that has stretched out its tentacles – westward to the Mallings and south to Loose (which I hate to mention again), though Linton just beyond it is little altered; the former Mann-Cornwallis estate has acted as a buffer. The different parts of the straggling parish of Boughton

said about Addington and Kemsing. What little there is to say about Leybourne can come in here; Hollingbourne too.

So now I have a few more villages to describe in this chapter, and a pretty mixed bag they are; some are real commuter places, others right out in the wilds, and some

Monchelsea, next to Linton, vary enormously, a rough and ready dividing line between semi-suburb – with intermittent housing, industry, hospitals, and so forth – and the country being the road from Teston, through Coxheath to the Five Wents near Langley. South of that road there is a quiet rural scene round Linton, Boughton church and Wierton. Going further along our ridge beyond Chart Sutton (near Five Wents) you move out of the strong Maidstone influence into its most picturesque and natural tracts, where lie Sutton Valence, East Sutton, Ulcombe, Boughton Malherbe and Egerton. We end at Great Chart, on quite a good note, the main Ashford–Hastings road notwithstanding.

If I had to choose I would say that in these hills Oldbury, near Ightham, is the most historic place, Linton church the most unusual, Boughton Malherbe the most peaceful, and Sutton Valence the most charming.

I will start then at Ightham. The centre of the village is most attractive with a curve in the road, the fifteenth-century Town House and other half-timbered buildings. A petrol station jars; this however is nothing compared with the dreadfully heavy traffic that used to ruin Ightham until the A25 bypass was made. Unfortunately the Gravesend–Tonbridge route still leads through the village. Ightham's best-known attractions are some distance away, the Iron Age fort at Oldbury hill, enclosing within its mainly earthen ramparts an area of over 120 acres, and the medieval manor house of Ightham Mote.

I feel quite unable to do justice, in my halting cadences, to the Mote. Why, I wonder, is it so spelt when it has an actual *moat* with enormous goldfish in it, and was spelt 'Moat' in the eighteenth century? It is built of ragstone, as you would expect, with some half-timbering and roofs of mellow Kent tiles. It stands fourquare with mullioned windows overlooking the water, dates back to the fourteenth century or earlier and is beautifully preserved; the interior is as exciting as the outside. The surroundings, woods and hills, and the approach, a quiet winding road, are all worthy of it. Pages and pages have been written about it; how lucky we are who live near enough to pay it a visit.

At one time the family of Selby owned Ightham Mote. They have brasses and memorials in the church of which the most striking commemorates (as our WI friends will know) a woman, Dorothy Selby, who died in 1641, a paragon of all the virtues, who uncovered a dastardly popish plot which would have shaken Britain to its foundations.

Down the Tonbridge road from Ightham is the Georgian seat of Fairlawne, whose two-storey-front towards the road, though mostly window, is faced in

131

Plaxtol

ragstone. The well-known Vane family lived at Fairlawne and one of them, Henry Vane, an embittered enemy of Charles I, was convicted of high treason and executed when Charles II was restored. The Merry Monarch, or his advisors, paid Henry the back-handed compliment of esteeming him too important and

dangerous a man to be included in the amnesty which was extended to the majority of those who had supported Parliament against the monarchy.

Nearby, the little village of Plaxtol straggles attractively in the last folds of the quarry hills before the Weald; near to it, along a very narrow lane, is the thirteenth-century stone building known as Old Soar, owned by the National Trust; it is in effect one end of a stone-built hall-type house. It will be remembered that the great hall was in the middle of these houses, with storied annexes at each end. On the site of the hall there is now an eighteenth-century farmhouse, and Old Soar, attached to it, consists of the Lord's solar, or drawing room, chapel and garderobe, with a barrel-vaulted undercroft beneath.

Moving eastwards from Ightham, and with deep apologies to Borough Green and Platt, which have almost nothing ancient, and very little modern worth exploring, I must make Offham my next port of call. We are now in what one might call the Malling complex where some of the old villages are quite submerged in the modern streets and factories, while others have survived remarkably well as islands, little altered. Of such is Offham; its green is not large, but has the famous quintain. There are up-and-over garage doors and television aerials, but they are unobtrusively installed.

The houses keep the old atmosphere, timber framed some of them and tile-hung. I have never heard of quintain surviving anywhere else; the word suggests medieval knights jousting at a swinging board but this one was used for local amusement by the youth of the village who, on horseback, took a swipe at the board and, if they managed to connect, had to duck the bag of sand which swung round to hit them.

Of the two Mallings, East Malling used to be the more important but now it is the other way round. East Malling is still a village, West a small town with a wide High Street and many Georgian houses, including quite a collection of them at the top of the hill, where the church is on the right. The only recent house in this part of the town is one immediately beside the churchyard – a little bit of sheer suburbia in the wrong place. In the church you can see that the arcade is neo-Gothic by the sort of vertical piece breaking the curve of the arches – even I can spot that. There is an eye-catching Jacobean tomb in the chancel on the south side – Sir Robert Brett and his wife. Whether the figures are stone, alabaster or just plain plaster they are painted, and the colours have been recently renewed.

Beyond the church you plunge into a well-heeled sort of scene – stately trees, large old houses, immaculately kept-up Wealden gem, ornamental lake at the wayside,

Offham quintain

and, in the midst, the Norman ruin called St Leonard's Tower. Further on is the old RAF station. No planes fly from there now, but thirty years ago its fighters were deciding the fate of the world, and all over the globe the name West Malling can stir the memories when survivors meet.

133

Back to earth, the famous abbey is along one side of Swan Street, the road leading to East Malling. It has an ancient gatehouse, and within, overtopping the gatehouse and surrounding trees, is a large ruined tower which has a distinct family resemblance to pictures of St Ethelbert's Tower at Canterbury before it fell. Many modern buildings are built on to the ancient ones to house the forty nuns who now inhabit the abbey. I only hope their library does not include a copy of Lambarde's *Perambulation* in which he makes such scandalous insinuations against the medieval predecessors of the present nuns. The "Abbay of women" founded by Bishop Gundulph in the eleventh century was suppressed at the Reformation, but that did not stop Lambarde from suggesting that their nunnery had been founded so that the monks of Rochester "might have a convenient place to resort to ... " (Out of respect for Kentish womanhood I refuse to quote the rest.) One must make allowances, I suppose. In those days, although these was a queen regnant on the throne of England at its most brilliant period, nevertheless in private life a woman only came to the notice of the Lambardes of this world if she had exceptional beauty like Joan, the Fair Maid of Kent, whom the Black Prince married, or exceptional possessions like Juliana de Leybourne, who was so rich that they called her the Infanta of Kent. This expression might not inappropriately be translated 'poor little rich girl', for Juliana, though thrice married, had no family, and on her death her great estates escheated to the Crown for want of heirs. Perhaps the air of Leybourne is not as stimulating as that in other parts of Kent – Eastwell, for instance, where (much later) the second Earl of Winchilsea lived, who had in all twenty-seven children by four different wives.

East Malling is beset with modern stuff, but manages to keep its integrity as an old-time Kent village. If there were any doubt about this, the Wealden hall-type house on the road leading to the ancient church would remove it. Practically the whole of the right-hand side of the road leading back to the main A20 is taken up by the frontage of the Agricultural Research Station. The magnificently preserved mansion of the extinct Twisden family, Bradbourne, is right in the middle of this large estate given over to field experiments, laboratories and such. The house itself is used for offices, and the former stables as a library. The Twisden family portraits are kept in the main house.

The old highroad to London is a little quieter since they made the M20 motorway running alongside it a little to the north. Trapped between the two routes to London are Leybourne and Addington. The great family de Leybourne, one of whom was the famous Juliana,

East Malling

strange pronunciations belt where Ightham is pronounced 'Item' and Wrotham pronounced 'Rootem'. There are more stones near Trottiscliffe and at Birling we have the influence of the Nevill family, whose helmets and coats of arms almost monopolize the walls of the chancel and whose ladies carved the Gothic-style font cover in the church. The Nevills, who still have representatives in the parish, are descended from the family that produced Warwick the Kingmaker.

Maidstone, our county town, though something of a disappointment as the Kentish Babylon, is a good shopping centre, and it does have pleasant places around it, some of which are on the quarry hills, Loose (it will crop up), Otham and Linton for instance. Loose is almost a suburb, but is still attractive with the houses hugging the steep sides of its valley, and the main road carried over the local one on a bridge.

About a mile further down the same road is Linton, which has the famous Place, built in the eighteenth century by the Mann family, one of whom was a friend of Horace Walpole, who often visited Linton. Standing on rising ground, white painted against the dark surrounding trees, it can be seen for miles. In the north aisle of Linton church is the Mann chapel. The effect of entering it is similar to that of going into the sculpture room at the Royal Academy. All around, tastefully

have left fragments of their castle which has been converted into a great house, and relics in the church.

Addington's megaliths we have heard about already.

On the far side of the motorway are Trottiscliffe, Ryarsh and Birling. Mention of Trottiscliffe, which is pronounced 'Trossley', reminds me that we are in the

135

arranged so as to create no clutter, but rather so that each individual item can be properly enjoyed, are sculptures, several of them quite famous, commemorating members of the Mann and Cornwallis families. Galfridus Mann has a marble urn and Gothic arch all paid for by Horace Walpole; a magnificently executed reclining statue of a young man is the memorial for Charles James Mann, Viscount Broome, who died in 1835. Tablets, obelisks and mourning figures abound, and everything is kept spotlessly clean; one comes away very thoughtful.

Next door to Linton the parish of Boughton Monchelsea has no single centre. There are Boughton Mount, Boughton Quarries, Boughton Green, Boughton Place and Boughton Bottom scattered over a couple of miles. The most picturesque part is the Dell, near the old quarries. The abandoned workings are eroded by time and masked with disorderly scrub, and make a romantic setting for houses, old, new, expensive or intimate, some isolated, some in small groups, amid a little maze of corkscrewing and plunging lanes. This is all on the Maidstone side of the strategic Coxheath road; Boughton church is over a mile south in more countrified surroundings. It is an unusual building – it has the tower and its bells amidships, so that between nave and chancel the bell pulls hang down; they can be, of course, looped back, but would still be in full sight of the congregation. There is nothing against this but it is, to coin a phrase, a new one on me!

I have already promised to say something here about Hollingbourne, which falls between the two stools of hill and down, and we had better add to the list Leeds Castle in that same vale on the River Len. The village of Leeds and the site of the famous priory are about a mile away, and actually on the quarry hills. When I think of all the interesting things there are in Hollingbourne I know that I cannot begin to do justice to it. The Pilgrims' Road runs through, and many fine old houses are strung out along the road leading over the Downs to Tunstall and Sittingbourne, Hollingbourne Manor and Hollingbourne House, the King's Head and the Old Forge to name only a few. About a mile away is Greenway Court, once the home of the Culpeper family, who have many monuments in the church. The most spectacular commemorates Elizabeth who died in 1638; she is sculptured in pure white marble. But the most famous possession of the church is the Culpeper altar cloth, made by the four daughters of the family during the Commonwealth, to while away the time until the king should be restored. It is worked in gold thread and is one of the acknowledged wonders of Kent.

I will not listen to those critics who say that when you get close to Leeds Castle it is not as romantic as it looks

Leeds Castle

from the main road. It is a medieval fortress of many towers and battlements, on an island in the middle of a lake, and it goes back to the Norman Conquest. I hear there was a castle there in the tenth century but the Danes destroyed it. Robert de Crevequer built a chapel for three canons but he must have got tired of having the church breathing down his neck and so in 1119 he founded Leeds Priory about a mile away and moved them over. The priory developed into one of the richest monasteries in the county but there is absolutely nothing of it left above ground. To keep on the right side of the king a later owner, William de Leyborne, handed the castle back to him and the king had to appoint governors to look after it. This was the occasion of the trouble between the rich Lord Badlesmere and King Edward II that I have already mentioned. Since that day the castle which has, amongst other things, a very charming nine-hole golf course, has passed through many hands, and is now by the bequest of the late Lady Baillie, held for the nation by a charitable trust.

And now, back to the quarry hills and Sutton Valence. Neither the church nor the buildings of the public school make me wildly enthusiastic, but there is something about the place, particularly in the spring, that puts you under a spell. Hereabouts the quarry hills are more recognizable, rising up to four or five hundred feet, and so giving views across the Weald that are simply superb. Sutton Valence's attractive buildings rise from the plain in tiers, with the usual accompaniment of white railings guarding the roads, and narrow alleys with steep steps connecting one with another. Although the Maidstone–Tenterden road runs through, the town spreads out at right angles to it and fifty yards from the road utter peace reigns.

East Sutton, about a mile away, is only a tiny hamlet, but it has the same lofty perch and the same view over the Weald as Valence. The churchyard and the Park, where the old seat of the Filmer family is used as a girls' borstal, are beautifully kept up; the staff at the Park (who guard the keys of the church as well) tell me that they have a very high success rate: the beauty of this part of Kent melts the heart of any but the most determinedly refractory borstal trainee. In the church – do not think I am exaggerating – is the funerary brass to eclipse all other funerary brasses, of large size, of lively execution, and so far as one can see as perfect as the day it was installed. The deceased is Sir Edward Filmer, who died in 1629, and he is depicted with Lady Filmer and, below, their nine sons and nine daughters. The brass is seven feet long.

In most villages of Kent, the most interesting as well as the most prominent building is the church, and a description, of any length, of Kentish scenery becomes almost literally a 'steeplechase'. In the present canter across the countryside we have now three more fences before the finish at Great Chart – Ulcombe, Boughton Malherbe, and Egerton.

At Ulcombe the church is at the top of the hill, overlooking the modernized village and the Weald beyond. The St Leger family, who long held sway at Ulcombe, had connections with Ireland. They came over with the Conqueror, but one of them jumped off ahead of him and supported his hand as he stepped ashore. Much later on, in the reigns of Henry VIII, Edward VI and Mary, in fact, Ralph St Leger was lord deputy of Ireland: "and being well versed in Irish affairs, he by his prudence and magnanimity did more towards civilising that nation and alluring it into a submission to the English government than any one had done since the conquest of it to his own time." A Tudor 'Willie Whitelaw' in fact. But his son (called Warham St Leger from a connection with William Warham, archbishop of Canterbury) was less fortunate in that same island; he was appointed chief governor of Munster in 1556 and "performed eminent services for her majesty in the progress of which he was unfortunately slain in 1599 at the head of his troops in an encounter with Hugh Macquire and his followers, the two chiefs killing each other in combat.

Sutton Valence

The ridge now becomes much more distinct – my map tells me that it rises to 500 feet or more – as we approach Boughton Malherbe. The country round here is quite unspoilt, the roads narrow and some of the signposts a little confusing. It is a great place to explore, right off the beaten track, up hill and down dale, woodlands

139

alternating with broad fields; the North Downs are there to see in one direction, the Weald in the other. Boughton Malherbe, a glorious name, has Chilston Park half in and half out of its parish and is ringed with places that cry out to be investigated – Sandway, Platt's Heath and Grafty Green. Again the church is on a hilltop, next to what remains of Boughton Place, former home of the Wotton family. They came here soon after the time of Richard II, and of them it is said that "for their learning, fortune and honours at times when honours were really such, [they] may truly be said to have been ornaments to their country in general and to this county in particular." This great and distinguished family sprang from a draper who was twice lord mayor of London. Their descendants included Nicholas, the first dean of Canterbury, who was also dean of York (at the same time), another Nicholas, a famous diplomatist, and the celebrated Henry, an author as well as a diplomatist, who was responsible for the saying (about an ambassador being "an honest man sent to lie abroad for the good of his country") which so annoyed that humourless Scotchman, James I. In the church there are many monuments, both brasses and effiges, of this very distinguished family.

In the time of the Stuarts the Stanhopes obtained Boughton Malherbe by marrying into the Wotton family, and some of them changed their name to Wotton. Not so Philip Dormer Stanhope, who succeeded in 1726 to the title of Earl of Chesterfield; he was famous for his wit and polish, caustic sayings and letters to his son. He also distinguished himself as governor of Ireland, where his administration is described as brilliant. Eventually this family sold out to Galfridus Mann, ancestor of Horatio Mann of Linton, who changed his name to Horace to distinguish himself from another Horatio Mann.

In this same countryside is Egerton, whose church is one of the boundaries of the Weald, and is a landmark for miles around with its characteristic little turret rising from the top of its tower. How often do we ordinary motorists see the fingerpost pointing the way to Egerton; how seldom do we follow it! Pluckley is a sister village, once dominated by a great family, the Derings of Surrenden, which house alas is no more unless you count one wing which survived the disastrous fire. The Derings too have gone.

At Great Chart my present task ends. I have skipped over the hamlets of Pluckley Thorne, Dowle Street, Ripper's Cross and Goldwell; some day perhaps we shall come back to them. Great Chart church has many monuments and brasses of the Toke family of Godinton House, and to the west is the court lodge acclaimed by the architects as a thirteenth-century building. External proof of this is only in the roof, the porch and the rear quarters; the windows of the front are in the Georgian style. In the churchyard there is a little timber-framed building called, I am told, the Pest House (what the people who live in it think about such a name I do not know). It is supposed to have been a sort of medieval isolation hospital, very handily situated for those patients who did not recover, who were probably in the majority.

Sissinghurst

141

CHAPTER TEN

'Wealdy' Kent

The adjective 'wealdy' is borrowed from Edward
Hasted, who has a great deal to say about the region, not
all of it consistent. "There are [sic] diversity of opinions
touching the true limits of this Weald," he tells us,

> some affirming it to begin at one place, and some at another,
> which uncertainty arises from its having been from time to time
> made less and less by industry, and being now in a manner
> wholly replenished with people, and interspersed everywhere
> with wealthy towns and villages, it may more reasonably be
> maintained that there is no Weald at all, than to ascertain where
> it ought to begin or end.

Yet when he comes to actual parishes he sometimes states
the boundary of the Weald very exactly — for instance he
says that Egerton church marks it; so I reckon that if you
stand in the middle of the nave of Egerton church with

your feet well astride you can say that one foot is in the
Weald and the other foot out of it! Sometimes they had
to know the boundary because the payment of tithe
depended on it; if your farm was in the Weald you
didn't as a rule have to pay tithe on woodland. Certainly
it comprises a large section of the county, and every
motorist travelling from North or East Kent to the
south or the west must traverse it.

For some reason the Weald, more than any other part
of Kent, seems to bring out the poet in people. Even the
staid authority we have been quoting got as near to it as
that authority's prosaic nature would allow him:

> The Weald, when viewed from the adjoining hills, which
> command a prospect over the whole of it, exhibits the most
> delightful scene that can be imagined. It appears to the eye an
> extensive level country (the few hills in it being so small and
> inferior to those from whence it is viewed), covered with all the
> richness of both art and nature, the variety of small enclosures of
> corn and meadow, and the houses, seats and villages,
> promiscuously interspersed among the large and towering oaks,
> which grow over the whole face of it, have the most pleasing
> effect, and represent to us, even at this time, something through a
> great improvement of its original state, in the idea of an inhabited
> and well cultivated forest.

This is not a bad description of parts of it as they are
today, but the modern generation of lady novelists and

poetesses[1] sings more sweetly of " ... miry lanes where the hedges blossom with honeysuckle and wild roses ... little woods with their funny names ... that are charred embers of local history ... In springtime the valleys and sheltered hillsides are bridal with blossoming orchards, and in autumn the air drifts with the smoky sweetness of drying hops." And again: "the dim blue goodness of the Weald."

Frankly, it is unsound to describe the scenery of the Weald in general terms, because it is as diverse, as are the Downs. The country round Hemsted Forest is as different from that round Rolvenden as the latter is from the surroundings of Headcorn. I like it as a place where I can still get lost; the vast extent, the meagreness of the signposting, and my own defective navigation have often taken me to beauty-spots that I never even dreamed of finding.

Most people know that the key to the character of the Weald is its name, which comes from an Anglo-Saxon word meaning a wooded place – compare the German *Wald*. Some writers use such adjectives as 'uninhabited', 'impenetrable', and so forth, but the more knowledgeable insist that Andredsweald, its old name, was in fact inhabited, albeit only sparsely, from Saxon

[1] Sheila Kaye-Smith and V. Sackville-West.

times onward. Before that it may well have been the paradise for deer and wild hogs (not to mention a Druid or two) beloved of the more romantic type of writer. A great feature of the Kentish Weald are the innumerable 'dens', Biddenden, Smarden, Benenden and four or five hundred more. Although inhabited to some extent, it was sufficiently wild and abnormal to be excluded from the usual feudal landholding system, and its function was that of a pasturage for hogs, manors in the upper parts of the county having their own little dens in the Weald. Thus, Tenterden was the den, or hog pasture, of the men of Thanet.

Over towards the Sussex border there are 'hursts' and 'leys', Goudhurst, Staplehurst, Sissinghurst, Brenchley, Tudeley and Willsley being examples. The experts seem less ready with their explanation of the history of these places, beyond emphasizing that they were not 'dens', but rather places where the trees were sparser, but even amongst these, and indeed over the Sussex border, the occasional 'den' is still to be found.

By what stages did the Weald evolve from a woodland feeding-place for hogs into the present settled, rich and prosperous farmland? The books I have read are not very explicit. By the time of Edward III it was evidently a place good enough to receive imported labour – Flemish weavers – so that by the fourteenth century the process of change must have been fairly well advanced. These Flemings were settled more particularly in the district round Cranbrook.

There was such a thing as the balance of payments even in those days. England was the great source of wool for clothing, but only the Flemings across the Strait of Dover were skilled enough to make and dye the higher grades of cloth. At this time in England we were becoming very fashion conscious; and swanky, brightly-coloured garments were very much in vogue; so Edward imported a sufficient number of continental weavers and dyers to start an industry here and to impart their skills to our lads. The experiment was successful, kept money in the country, transformed the Weald, and had interesting side-effects on conditions there. Many of the great families of the Weald, priding themselves on their genteel condition, originated as clothiers, an occupation that as gentry they would be quite ashamed to follow. It seems that if, even in some menial trade, you make enough money to join the ranks of the idle rich, then after a few generations you will be allowed to graduate to 'genteel' status. Some, however, would indignantly deny this, pointing out that at one aristocratic seat they still proudly keep the pulley that once hoisted to the loft the cloth required for making the 'gents' natty suitings'. The Kent gentry are if anything (it is contended) rather complacent about making money from trade and industry at the present time, and this is no new development in their attitudes.

What eventually finished the Weald off as an impenetrable forest (assuming it ever was one) was the coming of the iron workers who, at their peak in the sixteenth century, used stupendous amounts of wood as fuel. Names like Hammer Stream and Furnace Pond remind us that for hundreds of years the Weald was the Black Country of England. This is the expression of one of our authoresses, but she hurriedly points out that with wood used instead of coal it was not like the dreadful industrial areas in modern Yorkshire. She contrasts it in particular with the valley of the Swale, with its "smoking grimy towns and dreary mining villages, coke ovens and foundries and its stunted, blighted trees." Swaledale is in fact beautiful, wild and unspoilt, but I suppose we all make mistakes.

Cranbrook was again an important centre for a new industry and such delightful places as Biddenden, Tenterden and Goudhurst were once key points in this 'Black Country'. Perhaps Clergyman's Grey would be a better colour to use.

The clothing industry of the Weald waned, and finally closed down altogether because it would not modernize itself to compete with the new processes and methods that were developing in the hated north, and the iron foundries too proved to be incapable of holding their own against up-to-date coal-using competitors in other parts of the country. In any case the wood of Andredsweald was becoming exhausted – you must remember that to be of any use the fuel had to be very near the furnace; a haul of several miles would make it uneconomic. A socialist might say that the history of these industries is a case-book of the shortsightedness of the capitalist outlook – snatching at profits while the going is easy, taking the money out to subsidize a life of idleness and social climbing, and making no plans for the continuation of the industry when conditions begin to change. No wonder the workers of today try to guard themselves against similar vicissitudes.

The flat part of the Weald is noteworthy for the profusion of old timbered houses. The typical Wealden (or hall-type) house consisted of a lofty hall, open from floor to rafters with, at each end, a two-storeyed section of the same height. Obviously the plentiful supply of building timber – oak and chestnut – is the reason why there are so many of these houses, which make even the flat Weald interesting and picturesque. The High Weald towards the south where the ridge formed by the Hastings beds continues from the Ashdown Forest right into Kent is indeed what the poetess describes as "a

Biddenden gazebo

tumbled garden", with its many woods, parks and forests, and winding rivulets. Biddenden and Smarden are outstandingly beautiful villages in the flat Weald, and Sissinghurst Castle is on the edge of it; the High Weald has 'hursts' and 'dens' and 'leys' galore, with Cranbrook town as their focal point.

For those people who can spend half an hour looking

145

at a map, that of the Weald is one with which one can pleasurably travel in thought, flitting from place to place, so evocative are the names. Those of the seats and manors mentioned in old books are still there today, even if sometimes the buildings are new. The Biddenden–Headcorn area is particularly rich; Hammer Stream recalls the departed industries; a number of 'quarters' – Stede Quarter, Middle, Further and Waterman Quarters to name a few – are said to be memorials of Huguenot settlers. Whether the various farms bearing the name Nineveh in the Cranbrook area represent some past influx from the Middle East, I do not know.

Looking at Biddenden today it is hard to imagine it as an industrial place, but we are told it was a centre first of the cloth and later of the iron industry. I also read that in the eighteenth century a fifth of the population were Dissenters. A Free Churchman will be amused to notice how the old books constantly mention the presence of Dissenters almost as if they were telling you what proportion of the population had two heads. We learn also that the nearby village of Standen belonged to the family of Jane Austen the novelist, and that money left for the provision of a school at Biddenden was misappropriated, partly because the Archbishop of Canterbury as visitor showed so little interest in his duties as such. Most people know of the Siamese twins alleged to have lived in Biddenden in the twelfth century and to have left money for the provision of cakes bearing their image; the figures of these two maids in fact are the main feature of the village name sign. But research reveals that the story 'seems without foundation'. The truth appears to be that the money was the gift of two maidens of the name of Preston (the Biddenden maids were supposed to have been called Eliza and Mary Chalkhurst) and that the print of the women on the cakes only started in the eighteenth century and was made "to represent two poor widows as the general objects of a charitable benefaction".

Biddenden, with its many old houses and fine church, is undoubtedly one of the star attractions of the Weald, and is praised both by the romantic type of writer and the more technical. One of the former "knows of no lovelier village view than Biddenden seen from the Headcorn road", while the hard-boiled architectural critic says that at first sight it seems perfect to the verge of phoniness, too like a travel poster, but is nevertheless genuine. It is familiar to many because it is an important road junction; the ways lead to Tunbridge Wells, Ashford, Maidstone and Tenterden. Outside the village street is the Old Cloth Hall that fascinates me with its seven gables. It is the place where some of the cloth was made, not just a dwelling for the weavers, or their masters.

The church, particularly the interior, would interest even a Free-thinker. How the eighteenth-century and early nineteenth-century Anglicans could inherit such buildings – dating from Saxon times and bearing the imprint of every age since – and regard them (as some did) as sources of revenue and nothing more, I cannot understand. Things are different now and the church is beautifully looked after. I am intrigued by the three different types of roof, of the nave and the two aisles. The north aisle has a wooden ceiling with moulded beams; the nave has tie-beams and kingposts (with no ceiling); and the south aisle has tie-beams without kingposts.

Below, a long series of brasses from 1499 onward give interest to various parts of the church. All are on the small size, some are on view, others under carpets, sometimes rolled back when students come a-rubbing. But in the churchyard near the porch is a small new gravestone in the form of an open book, which remains in my memory more clearly than the ancient memorials within: it bears the name of a young mother and her five children between the ages of two and nine. What terrible catastrophe this records I have never had the heart to enquire.

Smarden

The country round Biddenden fairly bristles with timber-framed houses, Castweazel, Worsenden, Lashenden, Birchley, Standen and Vane Court among them. One could write a complete chapter on the village and its surrounding parish.

Another beautiful village in the flat part of the Weald is Smarden. It has only a secondary road running through it, so it is quieter than Biddenden. Every time I pass that way I determine that the next time I will stop and really look round, but something has always seemed to prevent me until a month or two ago. I first had a look at the church, and as luck would have it was disappointed. One of the ways to the churchyard is through an archway beneath a timbered building, and gives some feeling of entry into a precinct as the impressive bulk of the church bursts upon one. But alas, I could not see the inside. It had been temporarily stripped so that the roof could be repaired; it is supported by scissor-beams because of the exceptional wideness of the span, the nave being aisle-less. A slippery scramble and technical trespassing are needed in order to see the unusual type of bridge carrying the main road over the River Beult; contrary to usual engineering practice and due no doubt to ecclesiastical inspiration, it is in the form of two sharply pointed Gothic arches. One unassuming little building captured my fancy, a white-painted, clap-boarded cottage simply smothered in brilliantly flowering wistaria.

Most people who want a sight-seeing run tend to make for the really hilly part, the High Weald. Here, Brenchley is virtually another Biddenden but on an eminence which gives it added charm. Between the lovely old houses you have vistas of hill and dale. The usual picture of the church through its avenue of yews gives the impression that it is in the heart of the countryside, and it is a surprise to find it tightly enclosed in an elbow of busy road, bringing the traffic almost to the church door.

I suppose Cranbrook is regarded as the capital of the High Weald. Quite certainly a country town and not a mere village, it is another potential chapter-filler. The church is like a little cathedral; I like a bit of colour myself, so I think it was a good idea, and brightened up the church, when the descendants of the Roberts of Glassenbury had replicas made of the fancy heraldic coat and flags (officially called tabard and banderoles) commemorating one of their ancestors and consigned the faded originals to glass cases – just like the Black Prince's achievements in Canterbury Cathedral. But the rather blatant advertising of the old squirearchical families is rather overdone – grandiose tombs and monuments when poor people were probably going hungry! Over the church clock is an effigy of Father Time and they say that every time he hears the clock strike midnight he comes down and mows the churchyard with his scythe; putting another poor working man out of a job, I suppose.

One of Cranbrook's greatest treasures is the Union windmill; although it only dates from 1814 they spend a

Cranbrook

lot of money in keeping it up and in working order. The last time I was there one was unable to look over the mill because the contractor's men were giving it another doing-up.

Then there is Cranbrook Grammer School, formerly called Queen Elizabeth's, though it already existed when she gave it a charter, whereby hangs a tale of considerable length. The older buildings near the churchyard go back to the early eighteenth century; the new ones are not impressive.

There is a lovely old hotel, and good shops, and all in all Cranbrook is a grand place to stop off, either for a meal and a rest or to spend an hour or two looking round. Like Biddenden, it has interesting surroundings, such as the great park and mansion of Glassenbury, the ancestral home of the Roberts, and in the other direction, just off the Benenden road, the hamlet of Coursehorn with the Old Cloth Hall nearby. When Queen Elizabeth I came to Cranbrook she stayed with the Bakers at Sissinghurst, and the clothmakers laid a pathway of broadcloth three quarters of a mile long for her to walk on.

The Weald is endless in its attractions, but the same is not true of the space we have to describe it and we are forced to be selective. One of my favourite Wealden houses is Rabbit's Cross Farm near Boughton

Rabbit's Cross Farm

Monchelsea; it is typical of the buildings that lend interest even to what would otherwise be perhaps the duller part of the Weald.

Four 'dens', perhaps over-familiar through their being astride the main Thanet–Hastings road, should certainly be mentioned – Bethersden, High Halden

150

(beloved by architects because of its all-timber church belfry), Rolvenden and Newenden. For some reason the theorists have made the last-named a candidate for the 'Anderida stakes', the competition to be identified as the Anderida of the Romans from which Andredswald was perhaps named. At first glance, a less Roman-looking place we have rarely seen, and the arguments from documents seem unconvincing. Newenden is the last village in Kent on this highway, a stone's throw from the River Rother. If, just short of Newenden, we turn to the right at the T-junction, there are a couple of 'hursts' that have not been mentioned – Sandhurst (*not* the seat of the Royal Military Academy of course) and Hawkhurst, in the heart of the most scenic tract of the 'tumbled' Weald, itself not very outstanding, yet famous in Wealden history as the headquarters of the 'Hawkhurst Gang'. They were a bunch of eighteenth-century desperadoes who were finally defeated when they decided to invade Goudhurst, where the forces of law and order organized by a gentleman with experience in the army (as a corporal) easily defeated them and brought several to the gallows.

Between Hawkhurst and Biddenden lies a tract of undulating, wooded country with Benenden as its centre, specially charming in spring when the apple trees are in blossom and bluebells are everywhere, luxuriating even in the unshaded road margins. At Benenden is the historic seat of Hemsted, now a school of which Princess Anne is an Old Girl. In the eighteenth century when old Sir John Norris lived at Hemsted his difficulties gave prominence to the bad state of the local roads which were "so deep in winter that he was forced to have his coach drawn to church in the common waggon track by six oxen, one before the other, as the only means of conveyance to it."

Rolvenden is another pleasant village in a parish which had formerly "the mansions of many respectable families resident in it, but they are now, several of them, converted into farm houses." Another insult to the National Farmers Union, but a remark that should have pleased the ghost of Edward Gibbon; in his autobiography he recalled that "in the hundred and parish of Rolvenden the Gibbons were possessed of lands in the year one thousand three hundred and twenty-six; and the elder branch of the family without much increase or diminution of property still adheres to its native soil". The ancestors of the historian of the *Decline and Fall* were, one supposes, the Gibbons who lived at Hole Park, a family of clothiers who had graduated to the status of gentry.

There are scores of other places that I could speak about. I suggest we end with Goudhurst, Scotney,

Scotney Old Castle, Lamberhurst

Tenterden, and Sissinghurst, which used to be considered part of Cranbrook parish.

Goudhurst has been compared to the hilltop villages in Provence, but I do not myself think the parallel is very exact; Goudhurst is so English with its Wealden timbered buildings, its plain, solid-looking church. It has family memorials, especially of the Culpepers, including one with wooden painted effigies. The historian notes the great longevity of the inhabitants in his day, which he puts down to their "being in great measure untainted with the vices and dissipations too frequently practised above the hill." Yet virtuous Goudhurst has no steeple on its church for the same reason that Wingham, in East Kent, has to manage with wooden pillars in its nave instead of stone ones – the funds collected for the necessary reparation were embezzled. Goudhurst again is but one star in a constellation of ancient seats and manor houses, notably Bedgebury, the home of the great but extinct Culpeper family, now a school, the almost too picturesque Scotney Castle, a medieval moated fortress of the time of Richard II in a woodland setting with an Elizabethan house built on to it, and on the hill above the present early Victorian mansion with its splendidly landscaped gardens sweeping down to the ancient ruin, and Combwell, whose owner in the seventeenth century was slain fighting for King Charles at the siege of Colchester. Without meaning to detract from the many splendid attributes of Goudhurst, I will admit that the reason why I stop there so often is the good food at the local hostelries.

And next Tenterden. What is it that gives this place a completely distinctive character? A photograph taken here, even of some modest little cottage or shop, seems somehow to be immediately recognizable as Tenterden. It is right on the south-eastern edge of the Weald. As late as 1509 the sea came to Smallhythe, a mere couple of miles away to the south, and Tenterden is a corporate member of the Confederation of the Cinque Ports, being a limb of Rye. It was a great weaving place from the fourteenth century onward. The historian gives a remarkable example of rapid accumulation of riches from Romney Marsh by Tenterden people: a grazier in fourteen years acquired sufficient to become the purchaser of an important estate, formerly the property of the Guldeford family "and other estates that rented at £800 per annum". Much of Tenterden's history is like that of other places in the Weald, from the building of great family seats in the neighbourhood to the regrettable arrival of numbers of Dissenters. There is one typical Wealden half-timbered building, now a cafe, opposite the eighteenth-century town hall; goodness knows how old the Wealden building is – some of its

153

Tenterden High Street

features date from *alterations* in the sixteenth century. It is not however typical of Tenterden, most of the older buildings of which seem to be Georgian, or thereabouts. I suppose I am a Philistine to say so, but I find the cataloguing of architectural details difficult to take in, and therefore uninteresting. I think non-architects

unconsciously appreciate the effects that the designer is trying for, but when these are explained in the form of Doric columns, Tuscan pillars, four-centred arches and so forth, they leave me, for one, cold. Yet I can see, in a general way, that the Georgian buildings of Tenterden are in no way monotonous; each has its individuality, and at the same time each seems to have something that says, gently but firmly, "This is Tenterden."

For me, the most attractive feature of the parish church is its dedication to my favourite saint, Mildred. The inside is gloomy, with a good deal of garish modern glass with hackneyed themes. The tower, a landmark from afar and impressive from close at hand, is said to be the finest of any parish church in the county.

Finally, Tenterden has one of the trail of Hales Places scattered about Kent in their scramble for riches and power by the now extinct family of that name. I myself know of three, at High Halden, here in Tenterden, and at Canterbury. In the cathedral city, the name applies to a district, the house itself being long demolished. At the Tenterden Hales Place (the entrance to which, a private house, is in Oaks Road next to the police station), only the old gateway and the garden layout are reckoned to be from the family seat, although some of the brickwork of the present house has a definitely Elizabethan or Jacobean look about it — very like that at Sissinghurst, which for me will always be the pride of the Weald of Kent.

Sissinghurst Castle belongs to the National Trust. Those opposed to the Common Market will not like the reason usually given for calling it a castle when it is in fact the remains of an Elizabethan dwelling-house, known locally in times of yore as Bloody Baker's House for reasons that will be mentioned in a moment. In the Napoleonic Wars, captured French sailors were imprisoned there, and they called it '*le château*' – every big house in France seems to be a *château* – and the name, or rather the translation of it, stuck. The sanguinary element in its old name came from the evil reputation of a former owner, Sir John Baker, who was said to have put Protestants to death in the days of Queen Mary. But his modern apologists say that these imputations are untrue, and Sir John merely trimmed his sails a little to the prevailing political winds but no more than other careerists of the time. In other words he was a Vicar of Bray, but no Himmler. The Baker family died out in the male line; the daughters' husbands had other interests and the deserted mansion was slowly falling to pieces when it was helped on its way to ruin by the destructive French prisoners. It came into the ownership of Sir Horace Mann of Linton, about whom we have already heard, and he hurried things along by pulling down most of what remained for the sake of the materials. The part he spared had the great honour of functioning as the parish workhouse for some sixty years. When this phase of its career ended, it was used by various farmers until 1930, when Sir Harold Nicolson and his wife Victoria (Vita) Sackville-West from Knole took it over. The remains consist of the entrance range of the house built by 'Bloody Baker' and the tower of the Elizabethan mansion erected by his son. The Nicolsons laid out that unique garden that is one of the wonders of Kent and indeed of England. They lived on the premises, too, but the garden was their lode-star, the husband responsible for the layouts and the wife selecting the plants and flowers. Knowledgeable people both from home and overseas often see in the flower-beds of Sissinghurst many varieties that they have never met before. The thought behind the scheme is shown in a succession of blooms from March to October, and the series of gardens within the garden, for roses, herbs, spring plants and white flowers, with lime walk and nuttery.

In an upper room in the tower Miss Sackville-West wrote her books. On a sill beside the stairway, four vitreous tiles spell out the name VITA – what could be more moving than this simplest of memorials?

155

Igtham Mote

CHAPTER ELEVEN

Seats of the Mighty

I should not like the reader to think that the title of this chapter was meant to be sarcastic. In point of fact my own feeling toward ancient seats and ancient families is little short of idolatrous, and I am an enthusiastic supporter of the National Trust.

But the tract of Kent between the Hastings road and the Surrey and Sussex borders has no geographical unity; it is part Weald, part quarry hills, part Downs and part Medway and Eden valleys, and the galaxy of great and famous houses and seats, many connected with eminent national heroes, is its uniform feature; hence the title.

The National Trust owns many properties round here, notably Knole, Chartwell, Chiddingstone village and Quebec House at Westerham, the home of General Wolfe. The Trust also controls tracts of country at Ide Hill, Crockham Hill and Toy's Hill, all on high ground overlooking the Weald. Penshurst and Hever, the other star attractions, are in private hands, as safe fortunately as those of the Trust itself, and are regularly opened to the public who come to see them in tens of thousands. Many other great and privately owned houses of Kent admit people, usually just to the gardens perhaps once or twice a year, while an even greater number the public never see; they are after all people's homes. But how lucky we are that concentrated in this little piece of the county at the western end are so many great and famous homes that the public can enjoy with so few restrictions. At the same time it is sad to think how many others have disappeared for ever. One reads occasionally great lamentations in the Press on this subject, usually with the implication that someone is to blame, but all too often fire has been the destroyer.

We have reason to be thankful that, for some houses – I can mention only a few by name – a modern use has been found under government, central or local, or big public and charitable organizations: Bradbourne is the centre of an agricultural research station; Hemsted and Cobham Hall, girls' schools; East Sutton Park (what a contrast, or is it?), a girls' borstal; Maidstone Mote, a Cheshire home for disabled servicemen; Mersham Hatch, a Caldecott Community house; Otterden Place has been handed over to a mutual housing trust; Lees Court, the Inigo Jones mansion near Faversham, the remains of

157

Surrenden, the Dering family seat near Ashford, and Waldershare Park near Dover, adapted as flats. Leeds Castle, too, should now be safe. Occasionally one hears of repercussions that come from the difficulties of running these large homes when they have remained private, and of the expedients to keep them going. Recently a Sunday newspaper amused its readers with tales of bed-and-breakfast guests at the old Roberts' home, Glassenbury near Cranbrook. Many other seats remain private and unobtrusive. We must be thankful that all over the county folk are devoting money and loving care to these ancient houses. Many Kentish readers will have had acquaintances who are doing this or may even be doing it themselves.

Some of the seats are invisible from the highway, or nearly so, like Glassenbury, or Godinton near Ashford, or can be glimpsed only from afar like Lees Court near Faversham. Others stand proud and prominent, as Linton, Fairlawne, Mereworth Castle, Somerhill, Barham Court (Teston), Ightham Mote and Leeds Castle. Quite a number of our great old houses are haunted by ghosts, especially if at some time in their history the owner has had his head cut off! All have their memories, although so often the old Kent families who built them have become extinct, as have the Culpepers of Bedgebury, the Darells of Calehill, the Derings of

Surrenden, the Hales of St Stephen's, the Twisdens of Bradbourne, and here in the west the Bullens (or Boleyns) of Hever. But glorious exceptions to this sad record are Penshurst Place and Knole.

Penshurst lies where the Eden meets the Medway amid a tumble of little green hills. The village has all the charm of a Wealden hamlet, some of it old and some not so old, but the not-so-old is so skilfully done (there is money here to set the most cunning architects to work) that our guides have to be so, so careful not to describe patronisingly as restoration what may turn out to be genuine fifteenth century. The church is unusual with its heavy castellated turrets. The road winds across the meadow to bridge the infant Medway and the ancient Place is half hidden behind the church and its own tall yew hedge. At Penshurst Place there is romance in the true, non-sloppy meaning of the word. Sir Philip Sidney was called Philip by parents in trembling fear of Bloody Mary and her husband Philip of Spain and their executioner's axe, yet is immortal for his gallantry and self-denial on the battlefield of Zutphen when he gave his life, fighting against that same Philip. Nearly 400 years later another Philip Sidney from Penshurst won the highest decoration for valour at Anzio. Before the Sidney family came to Penshurst there had been the Penchesters way back in the thirteenth century and the

Poultneys in the fourteenth; in the fifteenth century royal owners, the famous Duke of Bedford who carried on in France the good work started by his brother, Henry V, and the other brother, Humphrey, Duke of Gloucester, strangled on the orders of the Lancastrian virago, Margaret of Anjou. Then there were the Dukes of Buckingham until one of them fell out with Henry VIII with the usual fatal consequences.

What have we come to see at Penshurst Place? The roses in their geometrical enclosures of box surrounding the lily pond, the herbaceous borders, the historic nut garden, the castellated mansion with its beautifully restored state rooms and galleries? All these, yes, but eclipsing them is the great hall, described by some as the baronial hall, fourteenth century and unique in all England, a huge structure sixty-two feet long with a roof "of rare devise" supported on what the layman might describe as a series of wooden arches over which are cross-beams, and kingposts holding up the ridge. These arches – richly moulded, as are the timbers running lengthways, the wall-plates and the purlins – are of chestnut and seem to spring from carved wooden figures. Between the Gothic windows can be seen the shadowy outline of wall paintings of men-at-arms. How much would it cost to put in such a roof today, and would the job ever get done? The fireplace is in the *middle* of the

Penshurst Place

hall, for when it was built chimneys had not yet been invented, or at least were not yet known in England. The rest, even of magnificent Penshurst Place, is secondary to this noble structure. Most important are the undercroft or crypt, and the medieval solar, now the state dining room. I cannot even begin to describe the displays of armour, furniture and pictures.

159

Hever Castle

In the village, the church of St John the Baptist, as one would expect, has its Sidney chapel, the third on the site which was rebuilt in 1820, but two famous tombs date from the pre-Sidney period, that of Sir Stephen de Penchester who died in 1299 and in death has lost the legs from his effigy, and the strange memorial of the 'Nun of the Albigensian Cross'. The Sidney chapel is a gallery of the arts with a striking and beautifully painted ceiling, in the form of a panelled tunnel-vault painted with Sidney coats of arms on a background of formalized trees. The best known of the family memorials is perhaps to Robert, the fourth Earl of Leicester of the period of Queen Anne, with two most fetching angels dancing beside the funerary urn.

A little higher up the River Eden is Hever Castle. A complete stranger may go through different phases of appreciation of Hever and its surroundings, especially the gardens. The first impression after visiting the Italian garden is almost certain to be that of having seen one of the Wonders of the World, but with a lurking thought that there is some incongruity here – conflict with the basic simplicity of the medieval fortified manor house converted into an Elizabethan dwelling that is the heart of Hever. The answer is given in Lord Astor's own guidebook of the castle and gardens. Its lucidity and frankness completely dispel any doubts as to the congruity between a medieval manor house and a renaissance Italian garden, the answer being that there is not supposed to be any. " ... the Italian garden ... " writes Lord Astor of Hever, "had to be situated far enough away to be divorced from the medieval castle and its Tudor garden." Moreover the guidebook makes no bones of the fact that the various Anne Boleyn and Anne of Cleves walks, smugglers' caves, and so forth, are not meant to be anything more than names for different features that are admittedly the creation of the present century.

The Bullen family came to Hever in the fourteen-sixties. In the reign of Henry VI like many another family they had used the mayoralty of London as a stepping stone to genteel status in Kent. After Henry VIII had taken a fancy to Anne Bullen and marriage was in the offing the lass started to spell her name Boleyn which was considered to be more refined. Everyone knows how this romance ended and that before the grim scene on Tower Green Anne had given birth to a baby who was to become England's greatest queen. The second Anne was the next wife but one, but when she failed to suit, it was her sponsor Thomas Cromwell and not she who quite literally got the chopper, while she as a divorcee had Hever to live in until her death. Thomas Bullen, Anne's father, has a magnificent brass in the village church at the castle entrance.

The castle itself is quite small by the standards of Knole, or even Penshurst, and the collection of neo-Tudor buildings in its rear known as the village was so created as an alternative to making additions which would be so large as to swamp the original. The

Chiddingstone

alterations that Mr William Waldorf Astor made between 1903 and 1907, after he had purchased Hever, included the diversion of the River Eden and of the public highway, and the digging out of the land to create the lake, not to mention the creation of an outer moat to supplement the medieval one whose waters had originally lapped the castle walls. The guidebook has a spirited account telling us exactly how the work was carried out with an army of eight hundred men, six steam diggers and seven miles of railway, and of the many gifted experts and designers whose services were requisitioned. The Italian garden is a repository for the outstanding collection of classical and renaissance sculptures amassed by Mr Astor when he was American Minister in Rome. I find the display of these ancient masterpieces amid our English flowers and shrubs most piquant. A sarcophagus enlivens a bed of irises; Roman senators look at you tolerantly across banks of geraniums and (more appropriately) valerian; Leda and the Swan are bowered in lavender. Archaeologists who have so often seen this last group used as a design on decorated Samian ware will look at it with casual curiosity, and the rest of the public do not give it a second glance. It is, of course, a hackneyed classical subject, but what a fuss Lord Longford and Mrs Whitehouse would have made if such a group had been sculptured for the first time today and exhibited in Trafalgar Square! The gardens of Hever are indeed an experience somewhere between the park of Versailles and the ruins of Ostia Antica, but still the most charming vistas are those of the old castle nestling amidst the woods, views for which the layout of the grounds has obviously been designed.

Hever is the centre of a triangle formed by Edenbridge, Cowden and Chiddingstone. The first-named is quite ordinary, but little Cowden is a pleasant maze of clap-boarded and tile-hung homes clustering round a church with a slim, shingled spire, a true bastion of Kentish rural modesty on the confines of 'silly' Sussex and opulent Surrey. Chiddingstone, in the opposite direction, owned by the National Trust, has that perfectly preserved street of ancient houses that, like Biddenden, is almost too good to be true. The present fabric of the church is not by Kent standards very old, the former building having been struck by lightning in 1624.

Chartwell, too, belongs to the Trust and lies in the quarry hills just south of Westerham. Within the modern building that was Sir Winston Churchill's home is the hall of an ancient manor house, though this is but little heard of compared to the wall that Sir Winston built, his desk and his library, the garden seat where he meditated and his studio with the finished pictures and the palette, easel, paint and brushes, half-smoked cigar and tumbler of scotch. Architecturally, Chartwell is a surprisingly unattractive house to be built for one who was amongst other accomplishments an artist. However, its situation is delightful with a glorious view over the Weald, and the emotional pull of its relics is perhaps best felt in neutral surroundings; the attention is not distracted. I notice, by the way, that in Sir Winston's well-stocked library there is a copy of Ronald Jessup's *Archaeology of Kent*.

Sevenoaks is so near to the Greater London border that it is, as you would expect, largely suburban, but it still struggles to keep a little of the small-town atmosphere. In St Nicholas's church is a monument to William Lambarde, the Perambulator of Kent, but the most notable buildings in Sevenoaks itself are those of the school, founded by Sir William Sevenoke, a foundling who had a successful Dick Whittington type of career in the City in the fifteenth century. Three hundred years later there was a great rebuilding, with Richard Boyle, Earl of Burlington and Cork, as architect.

But Knole Park and mansion to the south-east of the town eclipse all else; it is a National Trust property, but Lord Sackville still lives there. Often in the history of Kent, good has come out of evil; Knole gives us another example. One of the county's greatest and most magnificent treasures would not have existed but for the misfortunes already mentioned of the Fiennes family,

Chartwell

Lords Say and Sele. The father, James, as you will remember, had a most horrible end at the hands of the Cheapside mob, instigated by the rebel Jack Cade. His son got completely embroiled in the Wars of the Roses, and ruin was staved off only by the sale of the manor of Knole, which the family owned, to Thomas Bourchier, Archbishop of Canterbury. He transformed an uncouth medieval hotchpotch into an abode "fit for the princes of the church" and later for the Sackvilles. Archbishop Cranmer, to whom Knole descended, found to his dismay that King Henry VIII had his eye on it and after a desperate attempt to fob the King off with the Otford Palace the Archbishop handed the property over. Thus it was that Queen Elizabeth was able to make a present of the house to her cousin, Thomas Sackville, the first Earl of Dorset. The Sackvilles succeeded one another at Knole for centuries but in Victorian times the descent came down in the female line to the Sackville-Wests who are still there.

Knole can best be described as a rugged English forerunner in the tradition which was to find its culmination in Versailles. It is a huge palace of a house, sumptuously decorated and furnished, and adorned with innumerable works of art, including notably portraits with a strong family connection, the Earls and Dukes of Dorset of course; but for me the most endearing are two

Sevenoaks

ladies, Lady Anne Clifford and Lady Betty Germain. Anne was married to the spendthrift gambling third Earl and spent most of her time in a rearguard action to stop him getting hold of her own estates in Cumberland and Westmorland, where her family, the Earls of Cumberland, held sway. One would have thought that her relations with the Earl would have been pretty cool but their numerous children seem to suggest otherwise. Lady Betty Germain was a former lady-in-waiting of Queen Anne, and her husband had been a reputed son of William of Orange; but at Knole she was merely a friend of the family, a wealthy woman who lived there during her widowhood, but with the distinct promise that on

Knole

her death she would leave money to one of the younger sons. She seems to have been one of those characters who impress themselves on their surroundings and Knole will always recall her memory. The suite of rooms that she occupied is shown to people to this day, in series with the Green Court and the Stone Court, the Great Hall that Archbishop Bourchier built, various galleries, dressing-rooms and bedrooms, all lavishly furnished and adorned with paintings on many subjects as well as the family portraits, and statues, including one of Giannetta Baccelli, the third duke's Italian girl-friend, undraped. The pictures include copies of Raphael's cartoons from which the Cartoon Gallery takes its name.

During the last war, Knole had several narrow escapes: a 'Molotoff breadbasket' showered 700 incendiaries over it, but none fell on any vital spot; a parachute mine detonated just outside the main gateway, smashing hundreds of windows, but doing no major structural damage.

In the Park, within a short distance of the bustle of Sevenoaks, you can look in all directions and espy perhaps one building; it is a park in the original sense of an enclosure for deer. These animals are very tame, and approach motorists and others for food, even pushing their heads inside the cars if not handled firmly. One piece of information I can give, which I have not seen in any work of reference whatever: these deer will *not* eat pickled onions.

On the London side of Sevenoaks, Bessels Green, Riverhead and Dunton Green are suburban, and Chipstead half village and half suburb. Through this country runs the dual-track Sevenoaks bypass, and we are very near to the border of Greater London. What a surprise therefore to find, between trunk road and metropolitan boundary, a peaceful neck of the woods which could well be, from all appearances, ten miles from the nearest town. Such is Chevening, a hamlet rather than a village, whose church in true Kentish fashion illustrates by its memorials the history of the great house which is its neighbour. Elizabethan and Jacobean tombs of the Lennard family were followed by eighteenth- and nineteenth-century monuments of the Stanhopes, including the famous one by Sir Francis Chantrey to Lady Frederica.

The road to Chevening is a dead-end, and there are many notices warning that cars may proceed no further. A high wall hides all but the upper part of the house; but, road or no road, there is a public footpath to Knockholt, and if you follow it you come into an open field from which there is a magnificent view of the principal front of the house, a handsome Georgian pile formed by adapting a mansion of the Inigo Jones era.

This is the place bequeathed to trustees by the last Lord Stanhope as a residence for the prime minister, a cabinet minister, or a member of the royal family. As we have all read, the Prince of Wales has been nominated as the first resident. This magnanimous act was by no means the first one to bring a member of the Stanhope family on to the stage of history. Philip Dormer Stanhope, the celebrated Earl of Chesterfield, has associations with Boughton Malherbe rather than Chevening, but the third Earl Stanhope, Charles, and his daughter, Lady Hester Lucy, were Chevening residents who did well for retailers of historical anecdotes. Charles was a democrat, and had been elected to the House of Commons before his accession to the title. His tolerance of the French Revolution earned him the nickname of Citizen Stanhope; in House of Lords debates he made a name for himself as a 'minority of one'. He invented, *inter alia*, a printing press, a new type of lens, a thing called a monochord for tuning musical instruments, and calculating machines; but when the other daughter, Rachael, eloped with an apothecary, Citizen Stanhope failed in the test of his revolutionary principles and ordered her never to darken his doors again.

Her sister Hester found Chevening too quiet and went to become the chief of household of her statesman uncle, the younger Pitt, acting also as his secretary when he was

167

Chevening

out of office. She made a serious contribution to the running of the country by supporting so efficiently its prime minister in times of the greatest stress, and Parliament granted her a pension on his death. When she could no longer remain in the centre of the political stage, Hester became restless and emigrated to Mount Lebanon, from whence she exercised a despotic authority, based on her personality alone, over the surrounding parts of the Middle East, which she pacified by methods very different from those of Dr Kissinger.

Chevening is not unique in offering a haven of peace within a stone's throw of suburbia and main roads. Neighbouring Sundridge has another well-known house, Coombe Bank, now used as a convent, from which the main A25 road, less than half a mile away, is invisible. The view from there towards the church (which is on the hill beyond the road) is one of a peaceful woodland.

Further west, Brasted, and still more Westerham, seem to be marred by too much traffic and parking and one has to find the nearby seventeenth-century Squerryes Court to recapture the peace of the countryside.

Finally, I shall get into trouble with some of my friends who live there if I finish without saying anything about Royal Tunbridge Wells. Why it is 'Royal' I am not quite certain. Only royalty who gave permission for

Westerham, the Green

the title could perhaps tell us. Royal it may be, but hardly rural; it has the famous Pantiles, predecessor of all the pedestrian shopping precincts, the church of St Charles the Martyr, and its Rocks. From an historical point of view one has to commend it for keeping the eighteenth-century spelling of its name, while its parent, in deference possibly to Hasted's researches, has gone back to an earlier version – Tonbridge.

169

Tunbridge Wells, the Pantiles

CHAPTER TWELVE

The New Canterbury

Kent has a great and glorious military tradition. Its fighting men claimed the privilege — whether it would be thought a privilege today I do not know — of being stationed in the van of the English army, and at Hastings they fought almost to the last man. Some people, including apparently the Kent County Council, claim that Kent was not conquered, but did some kind of deal with William of Normandy. Is not this monkish fiction a slight on the memory of those who fell fighting so bravely against the invader?

In more modern times there were two county regiments, the West Kents and The Buffs, the latter having their depot at Canterbury. The Buffs were like the man in Shakespeare who in his time had played many parts. They started as trained bands of the City of London, the lord mayor's private army; in the reign of Elizabeth they were sent as volunteers (so-called) to fight against the Spanish in the Netherlands and so became a recognized formation, the Holland Regiment. When units acquired numbers, they were the Third Foot, a Regiment of the Line, with the nickname 'The Buffs' from the facings of their uniform. Much later on, regiments were linked with different parts of the country for recruiting, and The Buffs were named additionally the East Kent Regiment; at their peak, having earned the 'Royal' prefix, they were entitled The Royal East Kent Regiment (The Buffs). After World War II came reorganization, contraction, retrenchment — call it what you like — the infantry were cut down. First, the old Third Foot had to team up with the West Kents, The Queen's Own Royal West Kent Regiment, to give them their correct title, and become 'Queen's Own Buffs'. But this was only the thin edge of the wedge; the Queen's Own Buffs were in turn amalgamated with others to form The Queen's Regiment, so now there are no Buffs at all. The Territorial and Army Reserve outfit at Leros centre in Canterbury, though the name itself is a Buff battle honour, are simply part of a territorial battalion of the Queen's Regiment.

Old Buffs must take such comfort as they can from the fact that Canterbury, their home for nearly a hundred years, has managed to survive as a city a little better than they have done as a regiment. It seems to have been a rather tough morsel for the Whitehall ostrich to digest; like all others, the municipal corporation was swept out of existence and its former area was amalgamated with sundry other ones to form a new 'district', but such is the power of tradition that the city of Canterbury has been allowed under the authority of royal charters to resurrect itself and give its title to the new-fangled district. I suppose it is a sign of age that I find the new city a strange conception, a Canterbury that extends from Seasalter on the Thames Estuary nearly to the top of Lydden hill overlooking Dover, and from the River Wantsum, the boundary at Thanet, right into the Downs beyond Stone Street and Waltham. This new, rather flabby giant has sixteen times the area of the old Canterbury and it will take some time to get used to the idea that people who live out in the woods at Thruxted, or down by the harbour at Whitstable, can now say "I live in a cathedral city". But at least, with Her Majesty's gracious permission, the title certainly, and its traditions (we hope), will live on. I wonder why it was all done. The Whitehall bureaucrats lead a very sheltered existence, and their ideas of cathedral cities probably came from reading too much Trollope; they imagined that it would bring a breath of fresh air into the cloistered cathedral atmosphere if the Canterburians could be forced to adjust their minds to harbours and coast protection, oysters, pierrots and so forth in one direction, and farming and forestry in the other.

Looking at the terrain, the new city has a thirteen-mile coastline that includes Herne Bay and Reculver as well as Whitstable and Seasalter, extending then to include the valley of the Great Stour from Shalmsford Street beyond Chartham almost down to Pluck's Gutter near Monkton, and all between that river and the coast, together with the little Stour valley, and the downland six to eight miles south of Canterbury.

And finally it has Canterbury, as we 'oldthinkers' (*pace* Orwell) understand it, the city of Augustine, Ethelbert and Becket, as distinct from the one that Ted Heath and Peter Walker have foisted on us.

The old Canterbury knew the name of its chief magistrate in the year 708, long before there was a unified kingdom of England. It argued that its institutions were older than the English monarchy, or any of the great offices of the state; it had been a city from time immemorial, a county of itself, and a county borough efficiently run and with a bright future. But now it is gone, and it is no use crying over spilt milk.

The attractions of the coast itself — such as they are — have already been described, and there is not a great deal between coast and Stour. The woods are pleasant, the remains of the old forest of Blean, some now under the

Forestry Commission, whose gravel roads give you in Clowes Wood a walk of a mile or two over heathlands with scarcely a building in sight the whole time, and in Blean Woods a stretch of two miles of bridle road in complete solitude. The road from St Stephen's to Swalecliffe with a branch to Herne Bay through these woods, and the Roman road to Reculver, are good examples of by-roads giving a pleasant alternative to those red lines on the map. Many of the names of the farms commemorate old manors, but there is not much else.

The great wedge of downland on each side of the Stone Street is wooded and full of little valleys, very pleasant to explore. I should prefer it to the open downs further east — round Adisham and Womenswould — although I see in the eighteenth century Hasted praised them as being the real East Kent country:

> remarkable, beautiful and pleasant being for the most part an open champaign country, interspersed at places with small enclosures and coppices of woods with towns, frequent villages and their churches, and many seats with their parks and plantations throughout it; the face of the whole of it is lively, and has a peculiar grace and gaiety. It is an uneven surface of frequent hill and dale but the valleys though noble and wild are gentle. The prospects are on every side pleasing and delightful over this country, bounded by the surrounding sea covered with the shipping of our own and of every other nation, and at the farthest ken of the eye by the white cliffs of France.

Apart from the three fairly unobtrusive coal pits with their attendant mining villages this is a pretty fair description of the country today.

The only village on the Stour above Canterbury (unless you count Shalmsford Street as a village, which I do not) is Chartham, but because of the predominence of the huge St Augustine's hospital on the hill, and of the Wiggins Teape paper mill down by the river in the midst of the village, Chartham is very large and only half rural. In better surroundings the church would probably be one of the greatest attractions of Kent; it is a fine building about which the architects enthuse, and which laymen find impressive, but its fame is based on its brasses, and one brass in particular, that of Sir Robert de Septvans. It is a big, finely executed engraving, the fourth oldest in the country, and there are besides four other brasses, of the fifteenth and sixteenth centuries, and on one of the tombs a group by the sculptor Rysbrack.

Below Canterbury, Sturry, smothered in modern development, is virtually a suburb and, like Chartham, has lost its ancient character. The Junior King's School is at Milner Court, originally Sturry Court, which has an ancient barn and the remains of an Elizabethan dwelling-

173

Chartham

house built by our old friend Thomas Smith of Westenhanger, Customer Smith.

A few hundred yards down the river Fordwich, once the port of Canterbury, is a much greater attraction. For anyone who has never seen a rotten borough here is their chance to do so. Fordwich was disfranchised in 1883 and for once one has to agree with those who say that tradition must not interfere with progress; though a limb of the Cinque Port of Sandwich, Fordwich is little more than a hamlet. All the same, the sixteenth-century town hall is probably as famous as those of Manchester or Liverpool. St Mary's church is centuries older; it has a Norman tomb, box pews and generally an aspect of antique simplicity quite in keeping with the rest of Fordwich, where anything modern stands out like a sore thumb, such as the rebuilt inn ipposite the town hall, which mars what must have been a fine grouping of church, town hall and riverside inn. Another grouping survives – the brick-built hump-backed bridge, with the old house Tancrey on one bank of the river and the 'George and Dragon' on the other.

Our books praise the church's Norman tomb as being unique in Kent. For some reason they do not tell us of Edward Hasted's exploit in rescuing it when it "was cast out in the churchyard, where being soon likely to perish by being exposed to the weather" it was purchased by

Fordwich

Hasted and brought to the precincts of Canterbury cathedral where, in his day, it still lay.

The house Tancrey is a reminder of the estate called Tancrey Island which in Edward I's reign was the property of the family of Marins.

The Stour is tidal here; the deep water and the moored boats suggest river trips, and the riverside path hints at forays afoot along the banks.

175

Westbere, further down the Stour on one of those twisting wooded loop roads, is a pleasant surprise, with imaginative modern houses amongst the older ones. Below in the valley the splendid lake, on what used to be Westbere Marshes, was created by the noisy and unsightly activity of gravel digging, and now is dotted with sails at the weekend.

The Stour flows on its peaceful way; after threading between the Upstreet Scylla and the Groveferry Charybdis it will glide out of our ken at Pluck's Gutter; let us now look at the villages of the Elham valley and the Little Stour.

Barham is a big village, strung out along the main road running through the Elham valley. Its nucleus is the higgledy-piggledy old-world part on the hillside round the church and court, but these are not the only old buildings, as you would expect. In the reign of Henry II Barham Court was held by Reginald Fitzurse, one of the murderers of Becket. In one corner of the parish, which stretches nearly to the top of Lydden Hill, is Broome Park, the seventeenth-century seat that Lord Kitchener owned. It is one of the most elaborately designed brick houses of its period, and the most recherché (I cannot think of any other word for it) of all the great houses of the New Canterbury.

A large part of Barham is woodland worked by the Forestry Commission, while on the eastern side are Barham Downs over which the Dover road runs. There are many earthworks and historic tumuli here, and there used to be a very famous windmill which, however, was burnt down when men were working on its restoration.

A mile down the road from Barham two lanes debouch from a little waterless valley that runs far into the solitudes of the Lyminge Forest. Between and along these two is the hamlet of Kingston, its church and its tithe barn. Kingston is smaller than Barham and has an intimacy that Barham has lost. So near to Canterbury there was bound to be modern development, but it has been carefully handled. The church goes back to the eleventh century, but apart from that one single fact it is hard to say what is so appealing about it, but appealing it is. On Barham Downs in Kingston parish the county races were once held, and the King's plate was annually run for in the month of August.

To reach the next village, Bishopsbourne, the road is forced into a detour by the existence of Charlton Park. The house is dismissed by writers in a sentence as being a plain Georgian mansion, but has achieved recent notoriety as the place where a pop festival was to be held; the proposal caused a blazing row which occupied newspapers and television screens for several weeks and was hot enough to cause the project to be cancelled. A good deal longer ago the mansion was used by the Prince Regent as a *pied à terre* when paying court to Lady Conyngham over at Bifrons in Patrixbourne. There is still a Conyngham Lane in Bridge, but Bifrons has been pulled down; some say that it was no loss.

Bishopsbourne church is interesting, rather like Kingston, and it has, as well, a type of sixteenth-century continental stained glass that is a little unusual: medallions showing miniature scenes are surrounded by plain glass, and have a fascination of their own compared with the usual figures filling the whole window. Scholars and church people will already know that Richard Hooker, author of the *Ecclesiastical Polity*, was rector here for five years at the end of the sixteenth century, and has his monument in the church. Beyond is Bourne Park, a Georgian seat for which it has been a problem to find a modern use. It was at one time suggested that the new university should be built here; later Benedictine monks had it; now (1975) the 'Housing for the Homeless' appear to have their eyes on it.

We are all the time following the valley of the Nailbourne, whose erratic flow irrigates at intervals Bridge, Patrixbourne and Bekesbourne before transmuting itself at Littlebourne into a normal stream, the Lesser or Little Stour, and then wending its way to Wickhambreaux and Ickham. All these villages are picturesque, though Bridge is the great battleground for the juggernaut controversy. People have been killed and buildings demolished by the continental monsters which continue to racket through, despite protests, sit-ins, and questions in Parliament. However, a bypass is now definitely started and Bridge's agony may come to an end.

When the sixth Marquess of Conyngham died a short time ago his obituary recalled that in 1950 he sold for £3,000 twenty-eight thatched cottages at Patrixbourne, "the loveliest village in Kent", which had no shops, no public house, no street lights, and one pillar-box. It would be difficult to find in Patrixbourne today one thatched cottage, let alone twenty-eight, and there has been a neo-Georgian invasion, but the superlative is still arguable. The church is Norman, almost in the Barfreston class. The scene as you approach it from Bridge is of a road shaded by a wall of evergreens to the left, with a slighter screen to the right, behind which the road slews away to reveal a picture thus framed of a compact building with flint walls, sculptured doorway, tiled roof, squat tower and shingled spire. Like Bishopsbourne, this church has windows of the fascinating continental glass – Swiss work of the sixteenth and seventeenth centuries.

Bekesbourne has its attractions. Near the old church is a mansion which was one of the numerous archbishops'

177

Patrixbourne church

palaces, and associated particularly with the name of Cranmer. This village is a limb of the Cinque Port of Hastings, though what kind of ships were able to sail up the Little Stour with its minimum depth of about one foot, and the intermittent Nailbourne, we are not told. At any rate, it meant that at one time you could do almost what you liked in Bekesbourne because until the mayor of Hastings, fifty miles away, heard about it nothing could be done about any malfeasance. No wonder it became "an ungovernable and lawless place". Nearby is the old Georgian seat of Howletts, which has achieved a certain fame as an open-air zoo. It is strange on a quiet Kentish by-road to read a warning against the dangers of the jungle in the form of rhino, lion, elephant, tigers, gorillas, wolves and other beasts.

Littlebourne, Wickambreaux and Ickham form a group. In Ickham parish, but nearer to Littlebourne village, is Lee Priory, built as a private house in 1783 under the influence of the Gothic revival, on a spot where no priory had existed before, the name being entirely romantic. Here lived, at the end of the eighteenth century, Sir Samuel Egerton Brydges, who claimed that his elder brother was entitled to the extinct barony of Chandos as a direct descendant of one Anthony Brydges. The Chandos Peerage Case was a *cause célèbre* and the House of Lords decided that the

Brydges were in fact descended from a Canterbury grocer named Bridges, much to Sir Samuel's disgust, especially after all the trouble he had taken to falsify sundry parish registers, as was afterwards distinctly proved. Most of the old 'priory' was pulled down in 1952.

Wickhambreaux is our last village on the Little Stour unless you count the tiny hamlet of Seaton on its outskirts. It has most of the interesting features to be found in the other villages on this river and they are concentrated round a small green, with a water mill in full working order for good measure, so that the centre of the village, with the mill, the thirteenth-century church, Georgian parsonage and a handful of timbered cottages, epitomizes the attractions of this delightful vale.

The new Canterbury may be a strange creation, but the old one is still there for us to enjoy. Physically, it has not changed at all; it was a very small city, and may indeed have had something of the village about it, even before these extraordinary 'reforms'. It certainly has a green, and it would be a good idea to go there first. Lady Wootton's Green is nothing like the ones we have seen at Meopham, Offham, Wickhambreaux and other places; rather is it a little processional way from the city wall to the front door of St Augustine's Abbey, known as the

Fyndon gateway. Nowhere in the city can you see, in a couple of glances, more to evoke the different periods of its long history. Abbot Fyndon completed his masterpiece about 1307; when Henry VIII suppressed the monastery, and allowed most of it to go to rack and ruin, he preserved a small part for his own use as a staging point for continental travel. Thus it was that the gateway, remarkable for its sculptured turrets, has survived. In the room above the arch, Charles I spent the first night of his marriage with Henrietta Maria. On the left, a red-brick Tudor portal marks the entrance to the ruined part of the abbey which the saint founded with the encouragement of King Ethelbert at the beginning of the seventh century. This one look, then, has revived memories of the Saxons and their conversion, of the Tudors and the Stuarts. You have only to turn around, and the sight of the city walls with the cathedral beyond will provide many more reminders of the immense panorama of Canterbury's past. This is the finest remaining stretch of the city's ancient ramparts, with massive round and square bastions. Embedded in the wall are the remains of a Roman arch, though you would need rather sharp eyes to see them from Lady Wootton's Green. The fact that they are there proves that the present line of the wall is that adopted by the Romans, a theory that was reinforced when archaeologists were

able to dig through another part of the wall in the Dane John and discovered its Roman foundations. Almost opposite Lady Wootton's Green a small doorway in the wall leads to the cathedral precincts within; it is called the Queningate, meaning the Queen's gate, because here or hereabouts was the doorway used by Queen Bertha, Ethelbert's Christian wife, when going to worship at St Martin's. The bastions are solid evidence of the bargain made between the monks of Christchurch and the city authorities in the fourteenth century, under which, in return for a grant of land, the monastery became responsible for looking after the city wall. We even know which prior built which bastion – Sellindge the square ones and Chillenden the round. Overtopping the wall is the great mass of the east end of the cathedral, the choir, Trinity Chapel and Corona, with the Bell Harry Tower beyond, and in the foreground, the rooftops of Meister Omers. Trinity Chapel was built to hold Becket's shrine; the Corona is known as Becket's crown; Meister Omers, now used by the King's School as a boarding house, began its life as a monastic building. From this one spot, therefore, you can see symbols of virtually the whole history of Canterbury from Roman times onward.

Bell Harry thrusts his pinnacles heavenwards, supreme over his pygmy surroundings. Those of us who live or

Canterbury Cathedral

work within sight of him have come to know his moods – glowing ethereally under the flawless summer sun, brooding darkly as rain-clouds pile up behind his silhouette, prim and new-washed in the early morning light, heart-breakingly nostalgic in the rose-pink beams of the setting sun. Such are our illusions; let us keep them and let us disregard the officious probing of the over-scholarly, with their 'revelations' of half a million bricks concealed beneath that skin of stone; of the perfection of design being in part a mere accident that happened when Archbishop Morton instructed Henry Wastell to go ahead and shove an extra fifty feet or so on top of the completed edifice as originally designed (hence the strengthening arches between the piers of the tower, whispers the Tempter). Why, the scholars will not accept as anything more than a probability our cherished story learnt at our mothers' knees that the Harry in the name was Prior Henry of Eastry who died in 1331, and presented (as we thought) the great bell that Canterbury has heard ever since. Yes, anyone who pries into the archives of Canterbury Cathedral had better leave his romantic illusions at the library door!

If you enter the cathedral, as most people do, at the south-east porch, you can drink in the feeling of majesty of Yevele's nave. You must walk its length, mount the steps and go through the stone screen to enjoy William of Sens's choir and the Trinity Chapel. The guide will show the site of Becket's martyrdom, or the tomb of the Black Prince – I don't want to go over ground that is only too well known.

The most interesting architecture to me, in the sense that it is both older and less obvious than that of the nave and choir, is that of the Norman crypt, which is vast and quite incomparable, its gloomy grandeur relieved by its own carved capitals and sculptured columns, and by the perfect foil of the later and more colourful chapel of Our Lady of the Undercroft.

By what miracle so much Norman glass has survived when one knows what has been done to it over the ages – pieces turning up in America and so forth centuries after the smashing exercise by the Puritans – I do not know. The history of the cathedral glass helps you to understand why it is that the people at Brabourne are so proud of having some Norman material in its original window; it would be very difficult, if not impossible, to duplicate that claim at Canterbury cathedral, where the tale is one of switching the glass from one part of the cathedral to another. Let us hope that with the aid of the money subscribed by the public to the Dean and Chapter's appeal, the worries that every informed person must have about this incomparable heritage of medieval art will be finally put at rest. The most famous figure of all, Adam digging, has had to be taken down from the west window. This end of the cathedral has no street running past it, only the entrance to the archbishop's palace, but this fact did not stop the experts from claiming that it was the terrible fumes from road traffic that had caused, or at least contributed to, the deterioration of the glass. If they had pried a little further, they would have discovered that in the nineteenth century the Dean and Chapter installed gasworks at the west end of the cathedral, the effluvia from which rotted its fabric and statuary. Small wonder that the glass has suffered too! Our ancester Adam was first installed in the twelfth century in the choir clerestory; some of the patriarchs who accompanied him there went with him to the west window and others are in the magnificent 'portrait gallery' in the south-west transept. Of about the same age are the little biblical scenes in the so-called Poor Man's Bible windows in the north choir aisle; and only a little more recent, the windows in honour of Becket in Trinity Chapel.

How many vistors to Canterbury Cathedral understand that it was the church of a monastery? And how many realize that although the monastery was dissolved by Henry VIII, much of its fabric remains and can be seen to this day? Much has been made recently of the crumbling stonework of the cloisters; strictly they are not part of the cathedral at all, but a relic of the old monastery, its focal point in fact, where the monks lived when not otherwise engaged. The same is true of the chapter house; and the Green Court, now regarded as a perquisite of the King's School, was the great court of the monastery. The celebrated Norman Staircase was monastic, as well as many other nearby buildings still in use.

Speaking about Canterbury in the context of a book about Kent, one would be wasting time in describing features that are already familiar to most people, the Dane John prehistoric mound, the Roman pavement preserved in Butchery Lane, the Weavers' houses overlooking a branch of the Stour, the city walls encircling half the old city, and the Westgate.

It would be unhelpful to react against over-exposure by commending what cannot be seen at all: Cogan House, for instance, in St Peter's Street, has probably the best domestic interior in the city, but though fronted by a hairdresser's shop, is a private house. We therefore commend the nearby Eastbridge Hospital, founded, some say, by Thomas Becket, or, according to others, by Edward, son of Odbold, about ten years after Becket's death. The earliest parts of it, which are the hall and the undercroft, are indeed of the Odbold/Becket date when the hospital was founded to serve poor pilgrims;

183

Canterbury, St Dunstan's and Westgate

preference was given to those that were sick, those who were hale and hearty being required to move off after one night's rest. The chapel, which is next to the street, is in Decorated or in Early Perpendicular style; one writer says one; another the other. Is there any difference, one wonders. After many changes and abuses Archbishop Whitgift in Queen Elizabeth's time sorted out the hospital's affairs and set it on its career as a home for old people, which it remains to this day, with every modern convenience supplied, including colour television. But down in the basement the architecture is still that of the Normans. A little casement gives a low level view of the waters of the branch of the Stour which is called like the hospital – the East Bridge one. In medieval times the master of the hospital was responsible for repairing the East Bridge, which was only half its present narrow width, and the hospital and its garden were part not of the city of Canterbury but of the County of Kent and so remained until the Reform Act. Now, under the recent legislation, the hospital along with the rest of Canterbury is back again in the county.

A street in Canterbury well worth looking at, after the obvious ones of Mercery Lane, Burgate, Sun Street, and St Peter's Street, is St Dunstan's. This too was outside the city's limits in the Middle Ages, in the Archbishop's manor of Westgate, overlooked by the Gate itself, the finest in England, built by Archbishop Simon of Sudbury in the 1380s, just in time for Wat Tyler's rebellion.

A former mayor of Canterbury, one Francis Bennett-Goldney, took it upon himself to compose a monograph on the subject of Canterbury's most famous secular building. To add a spice of interest, he invented the fable that it was only by the casting vote of the mayor that the Westgate was not pulled down in 1850 to enable Mr Wombwell's menagerie to enter the city.

St Dunstan's is rich in seventeenth-century half-timbered buildings, no less than thirteen gables of them in a row, and on the opposite side the Falstaff Hotel. There are many overhanging upper stories, carved brackets and bay windows in such array that the street picture seems to absorb effortlessly the continental-type barriers and flashing lights of the level-crossing; they merely add an interesting twentieth-century dimension to the time-scale of St Dunstan's.

Beyond the crossing is the Roper Gateway, the entrance gate to the manor house of the Ropers whose name is so tragically linked with the fate of Sir Thomas More whose daughter Margaret married into their family. The gate is an elaborate composition of brick somewhat deadened by the similar fabric of the utilitarian brewery that was built on the site, but where no brewing takes place today. Higher up is the church from which the street is named, too old to have a certain date of dedication but known to have received Henry II when he came on his famous penance at Becket's shrine; there he dismounted and changed from what corresponded to battle dress into lowly pilgrim attire.

Here in St Dunstan's too is yet another example of good coming from evil. The present parlous financial plight of the country has at least resulted in the shelving of monstrous plans to dig huge tunnels under the fragile buildings and to leave the House of Agnes, seventeenth century and reputed to be the home of Agnes Whitfield in *David Copperfield*, trembling on the edge of a colossal abyss twice as big as the Dartford tunnel. The apologists *of course* guarantee that by some modern wizardry all could be carried out without harm to the ancient buildings, but the best guarantee of their safety would be the postponement of such scheme to the Greek Kalends.

Apart from its associations with Henry II and the Roper tomb containing Sir Thomas More's head, St Dunstan's church has little that is remarkable. It is modest in size and style of architecture as are most of Canterbury's ancient churches. Already reduced since the thirteenth century from twenty-two to nine, they are now being removed even more quickly from the active list. Of those that have survived to fairly modern times,

St Mary Bredman's was pulled down in 1900, Holy Cross had become redundant, St George's was destroyed in the blitz and not replaced, and St Margaret's is used as a church for the deaf. It is incredible to read that some kind of threat hangs over St Martin's, the oldest church in England. Surely, you would think, that should be kept going as a parish church at whatever sacrifice. St Peter's, which goes back at least as far as the twelfth century and perhaps to Saxon times, was united to the now defunct Holy Cross. It is still used intermittently and has a distinctly medieval atmosphere with its uneven floor, kingpost roof and even a little brass recovered from the ruins of St George's. It is now united to St Alphege, the church that stands practically in the shadow of the cathedral, and is possibly the church of the Crowned Martyrs where one of the early archbishops of Canterbury, Melitus, performed a great miracle by putting out solely by prayer a fire that was engulfing the city. St Alphege's vies in interest with the village churches of the county. It has brass of its own – not imported from some blitzed church – and until vandalism caused its removal, armour in the form of helm and gauntlets of Matthew Hadd, who died in 1617.

To the east of the city, St Martin's is very well known, and any brief description (which is all we could give here) would be totally inadequate.

186

We must not forget that Canterbury is the cultural as well as the religious capital of Kent, and it is now over twelve years since the university opened its doors. The massive buildings, which must rely for their appeal on bastion-like qualities rather than any particular grace or beauty, are ranged on the hill-top overlooking Canterbury from the north. The strenuous efforts to integrate Town and Gown have met so far with only moderate success. Physical separation can be overcome by mutual sociability, but this is not helped forward by the selfish, irresponsible antics of a noisy minority of the present generation of students. It was perhaps symptomatic that a faction amongst the governing body of the university fought bitterly to oppose a general move for the adoption of 'Canterbury' as its name, and clergymen of the other Canterbury in normally reasonable New Zealand had the effrontery, or perhaps were accommodating enough, to write a letter of protest at the idea of the city's using its own name for its own university! The same frame of mind was shown in opposition to the use for university purposes of the names of any of the saints and heroes of the parent city. Even the students were disregarded when they wished to have their college called after Thomas Becket.

These however are only the growing pains of a new, raw establishment.

But, wherever you wander in Canterbury, do not forget to look in some weekday morning just before eleven o'clock at St Michael's Chapel in the south-west transept of the cathedral, where from their glassy frames Methuselah and Enoch and their descendants look down on a brief but interesting ceremony that has been performed regularly for many years. When there were Buffs in Canterbury, the central figure was a serving soldier; now it is an Old Buff, parading in 'civvies'; his duty is to turn a page of the Book of Life, the old regiment's Roll of Honour of the dead of two World Wars. There is a brief religious service of commemoration, and many hundreds of watchers from far and wide. Whatever may have been the fate of our regiment, the Old Buffs intend to keep this tradition alive, and when they are all gone, there will surely be others, old soldiers probably of the Queen's regiment, who will continue the ceremony, perpetuating the name of the Buffs, and fulfilling the regimental motto:

Veteri frondescit honore

Their ancient honour is evergreen.

Index